MY
SON
DIVINE

MY

SON

DIVINE

By Frances Milstead
With Kevin Heffernan and Steve Yeager

alyson books
los angeles | new york

MANUFACTURED IN THE UNITED STATES OF AMERICA.

THIS TRADE PAPERBACK ORIGINAL IS PUBLISHED BY ALYSON PUBLICATIONS,
P.O. BOX 4371, LOS ANGELES, CALIFORNIA 90078-4371.
DISTRIBUTION IN THE UNITED KINGDOM BY TURNAROUND PUBLISHER SERVICES LTD.,
UNIT 3, OLYMPIA TRADING ESTATE, COBURG ROAD, WOOD GREEN,
LONDON N22 6TZ ENGLAND.

FIRST EDITION: NOVEMBER 2001

01 02 03 04 05 a 10 9 8 7 6 5 4 3 2 1

ISBN 1-55583-594-5

LIBRARY OF CONGRESS CATALOGING-IN-PUBLICATION DATA
  MILSTEAD, FRANCES.
    MY SON DIVINE / BY FRANCES MILSTEAD, WITH KEVIN HEFFERNAN AND STEVE YEAGER.—1ST ED.
    ISBN 1-55583-594-5
    1. DIVINE, 1945–1988. 2. MOTION PICTURE ACTORS AND ACTRESSES—UNITED STATES—BIOGRAPHY.
    I. HEFFERNAN, KEVIN. II. YEAGER, STEVE. III. TITLE.
  PN2287.D477 M55 2001   2001034113

CREDITS
ALL INTERIOR PHOTOS COURTESY FRANCES MILSTEAD UNLESS OTHERWISE NOTED.
COVER DESIGN BY LOUIS MANDRAPILIAS.
COVER PHOTOGRAPHY BY STEVE YEAGER.

I would like to dedicate this book to all of Divine's friends and fans in Europe and America and to the family members who truly loved him. You will always be in my heart and prayers.

Contents

As I sit down to write this, I realize it would have been impossible for me to ever have imagined the amazing journey my husband Harris and I were undertaking when the Lord sent our son Glenn to us on October 19, 1945. Like most new parents in the years just following the war, we wanted to have a quiet life with our children and to provide them with blessings we had not had when we were young.

Harris and I thought our son would grow up through the usual awkward childhood and teenage years, slowly finding his way toward things he enjoyed. We thought he might play sports or discover a subject in school that captured his attention, and that he would find a girl with whom he could start a family of his own. We weren't naive, though. We knew it would be a challenge to raise a son, and we knew that whatever we thought was in store for us would probably turn out differently than expected.

We just didn't know how differently or how crazy our lives would become. Still, we never felt anything less than blessed to have a child as truly special as Glenny.

In the many years since we first learned of Glenn's career as an actor and cabaret performer, we have come to know dozens of his friends and hundreds of his fans. Many of these amazing men and women have remained a part of my life. I have learned that Glenn had close friends in all of the many places where he lived—New York, Los Angeles, Amsterdam, London, and of course

in Baltimore. Since Glenn's death, these individuals have shared with me countless stories of the role Glenn played in their lives. Many of their memories inform the story of Glenn's life that I am now trying to tell.

As Glenn's mother, I am incredibly proud of the success and fame he achieved in his very short time on earth. Nevertheless, the story I am telling in this book is the unadorned and unsentimental truth about a sensitive child who became a very complex man.

It was very difficult to be Glenn's mother at times. He struggled throughout his life with many problems. Although he was blessed with many talents and abilities, he could be very moody and demanding. And while he could be incredibly kind and generous, he also liked to get his way. And he could certainly tune you out if you displeased him.

To complicate matters, in the late '50s and early '60s, when Glenn was a teenager, there were a lot of people, including me, who thought they understood perfectly what a family was, what a parent's role was supposed to be, and how a child was supposed to behave. Of course, the experience of raising Glenny, including the heartbreak of our years of estrangement and the joy of reconciliation, along with the incredible changes in people's attitudes and the blessing of knowing Glenn's extended family of friends, has helped me understand *family* in a totally new way. The wonderful outpouring of love I have received in the time since Glenn's pass-

ing shows what family really is.

But in 1957, when Glenn was being tormented by his schoolmates for being different, we had nowhere to turn for answers. Gay people were almost never discussed, and when they were, it was with off-color and insulting remarks. Those of us struggling with these issues in our families did not have resources like Parents, Friends, and Families of Lesbians and Gays (PFLAG) or the nationwide Metropolitan Community Church, both of which help gay people and their families

nowadays. We were totally on our own.

All this was about to change, though. In just a few years, lesbians and gays reached a new height of visibility, and anyone paying attention had to deal with a group of people who were, after all, our friends, classmates, coworkers, parents, and children. Much of the story that follows took place while all of this was going on, so I have included some of the more public events in the lives of lesbian and gay people as I became aware of them, mostly in the very unhappy years that

Harris and I were estranged from Glenn.

Many readers of this book will be familiar with *Not Simply Divine,* the currently out-of-print book written by Glenn's former manager, Bernard Jay. In that book, Bernard told many stories about Glenn's personal and professional life. I will not speak to anything Bernard says about Glenn's personal life, since Glenn was a very private person and did not share stories about his love life with his father or me, and we respected his privacy and did not ask. He never brought anyone to our house as his significant other, although anyone who was loved by Glenn would have been loved by us and always welcome in our home. All I learned about Glenn's love life I learned from TV. As for the stories Bernard told about Glenn's professional habits and his treatment of friends and coworkers, I have decided to let the people who knew Glenn tell what they remember. I'll leave it up to you, the reader, to make sense of the convoluted and sometimes contradictory story of Glenn's life.

Dozens of people have contributed to the writing and illustrating of this book. Many have been wonderful friends and given support in the years since Glenn's death, and many more have helped me fill in the details from his life during the time of our estrangement. I would like to thank my nephew George Gerba, Diana Evans, Sylvia and David at David's Beauty Salon, Valerie at Valerie's Salon, Buddy from Baltimore, Luis Lopez, my dear friend Pauline, Nancy Milstead, Doris Gent, my sister Anna, niece Martha, Alan Terl, and George Kissinger. To all the people who sent me cards and flowers, and who stayed friendly and visited me over the years—Jay Bennett, Anna and Vincent Spinoccio, James Lopes, Michael Shaw, Anthony Pierotti, Mink Stole, Jerry Stiller and Anne Mears, Steve Friedman, Mary Scarponi, Anne Cersosimo, Rebecca Hoffberger, Michael Blum, Donna Jean Cocoa, Michael O'Quinn, Donna Mance, John Shields, Greg Gorman, and Max Hager—your kindness to me will never be forgotten. A very special thank you to Reverend Higgenbotham and John Waters for the beautiful eulogy they gave my son. I would also like to thank the pallbearers who carried Glenn to his final resting place on Prospect Hill in Towson, Maryland, as well as Sharon and Frank Kujan, Spencer Cruz, Don McKay, James Ghani, John Waters, Pat Moran, Ricki Lake, New Line Cinema, Suzanne Juni, Andrew Logan, Michael Davis, Zandra Rhodes, Robyn Beeche, and Mitch Whitehead. And of course Kevin Heffernan and Steve Yeager, who spent long, long hours reading my handwriting, listening to my tapes, and looking at my photographs of Glenny to help me write this book.

Frances Milstead
Margate, Florida
November 2001

CHAPTER 1

"Divine. That's my name. It's the name John gave me.
I like it. That's what everybody calls me now, even my close friends. Not many of
them call me Glenn at all anymore, which I don't mind. They can call me whatever
they want. They call me fatso, and they call me asshole, and I don't care. You always
change your name when you're in show business. Divine has stuck as my name.
Did you ever look it up in the dictionary? I won't even go into it. It's unbelievable."

—Divine on the set of *Female Trouble* (1974)

"Why are you so nice to that guy Richard? Don't you know he is gay?" The two ladies crowded around me in the restroom of Univis Optical, where I worked. I looked them straight in the eyes, and they stared back at me. That made me angry, and I told them, "He's a human being just like the rest of us. If you had taken the time to get to know him, you'd see how nice and polite he is." The ladies looked at me like they didn't understand a word.

I'd met Richard in 1980, just a few months after he'd been hired by Univis. My husband Harris and I had moved to Florida in 1972 after selling our day-care business in Lutherville, Maryland, because the doctor had told us the warm climate would be good for Harris's muscular dystrophy. Harris spent his days fishing while I worked, and we spent our evenings together. I had many friends at Univis, but I was drawn to Richard,

a gentle, sensitive, and polite young man who was always nice to me. We ate lunch together often. Now here I was in the ladies' room surrounded by women telling me I shouldn't sit with him in the cafeteria!

These were the same ladies that had looked at Glenn's high school graduation picture hanging in our house on the living room wall and told me what a handsome son Harris and I had. I had never talked about Glenn at my workplace, though. Whenever someone asked if I had any children, I would answer, "Yes, one. He lives in California and isn't married." I felt guilty telling a lie.

The ladies would feel sorry for me on Mothers' Day because I never received a Mothers' Day card from Glenn. So they sent me cards to make up for it. They may have been prejudiced against gays, but they were nice people.

Harris and I had tried hard to help

Glenn get started in life after high school graduation, sending him to cosmetology school in Baltimore, opening a beauty salon for him, and supporting him while he lived at home. But he was constantly in trouble. He wrote bad checks, charged expensive parties to Harris and me, and was always very secretive about where he was going and who his friends were.

In 1972 we took away his car after he charged a major repair to us, and we told him we would not help him anymore. The next day he came by the house for his two little dogs and then disappeared. We did not see or speak directly to him for nine years, and the memory of the day he left is like a knife in my heart.

Richard and I continued our friendship, despite the women at work. One day at lunch I noticed he was reading a *Life* magazine. As I looked over his shoulder, I saw the name John Waters in an article about some strange movies being made in Baltimore. I remembered hearing Glenn say that name, and that Glenn had even brought this John Waters home to lunch one day. I wasn't there, but Harris told me that John had seemed like a nice young man, but he dressed weird. I asked Richard if he would give me the magazine when he was through reading.

He did, and I quickly turned to the page that referred to John Waters. A portion of the article read, "When Divine's mother found out that he was making underground movies,

she sold their home and nursery and moved and never told him."

I suddenly remembered, years earlier, finding papers under Glenn's mattress that appeared to be script or a play with the name Divine written on almost every page.

The magazine article definitely had my attention, so I turned the page and saw a picture of a large lady wearing crazy eye makeup and a red fishnet gown. Under all of the crazy makeup I saw two sparkling eyes that I would recognize anywhere: Glenn's. The statement about "Divine's mom" was referring to me!

Did Glenn really think we were ashamed of him? Was he afraid we would discover he was acting in underground movies? Since our estrangement, we had only heard from him on postcards giving no return address that stated, basically, "I am fine." Over the years, we had received postcards from New York, Los Angeles, Amsterdam, Rome, and London, over 50 in all. But he had never told us what he was doing or why he was traveling. How I treasured those postcards! They were pasted into an album that I looked at every day.

I was completely shaken up. I could barely keep it together enough to ask Richard if he would let me take the magazine home. I wanted to show the article to Harris. I never told Richard why I wanted the magazine.

When Harris read the article, he couldn't believe that Glenn was Divine and that he was making movies and getting his picture

would take me to see the movie. (I had been living in the area for less than two years and didn't know my way around Coral Gables. And Salvatore, whom we'd known in Baltimore, had been wonderful in helping Harris and me get settled.) Salvatore said he would take me, and our plans were made. Then I called Harris to ask if he wanted to go too. He didn't. He was not feeling well and told me that when I came home I could tell him about it.

As it turned out, Pauline and Denise, two of my friends from work—not the two who'd told me I shouldn't spend time with Richard—agreed to come along, first to dinner and then to the movie. When they found out that Glenn was Divine, they asked why I had never mentioned anything about him at work. I told them I didn't want people to talk and say things that would hurt me.

As I was buying my ticket, three men came up to me and told me not to see the movie because I obviously did not know what I was in for. I smiled and said, "I'll give you my opinion after I see it." Pauline said, "I don't know why she wouldn't like it. Divine is her son." When the three men realized we were telling the truth, they got a big kick out of it.

I couldn't wait to see what Glenn had

in *Life* magazine without telling us.

One day soon afterward, my friends and I had the radio on at work so we could listen to music and news, and I heard that the movie *Female Trouble* starring Divine was playing in Coral Gables just outside Miami. I got so excited that at lunchtime I called Harris's and my friend Salvatore, who was living in nearby Hallendale, to ask if he

been up to, but boy, was I in for a shock! Sitting in the theater watching *Female Trouble* was the first time I had seen Glenn in drag (other than the picture in *Life*). It didn't bother me, though. I watched the movie thinking he was someone else.

The movie was funny and some parts brought back memories. Several scenes were like crazy mixed-up versions of things that had really happened in Glenn's life. For instance, Glenn loved Christmas. As a boy, he would decorate our tree beautifully, and he played Santa Claus for the children at the day-care center Harris and I owned. Imagine my surprise to see him pulling the Christmas tree down on his mother in the movie because he didn't get the cha-cha heels he wanted! I even recognized one of the dresses he wore in the movie because I had found it in his closet in Lutherville. I had thrown it in the trash thinking it was a Halloween costume somebody wore. He must have fished it out, because there it was up on the screen! Also, the earrings he wore were ones he had given me in 1960 to go with a white gown trimmed with white fox fur that he had designed for me to wear to a Christmas party at the Tail of the Fox nightclub in Lutherville.

For me, the craziest scenes were the ones set in the beauty parlor. I have many memories of Glenn's years in the salon and the way he and his customers kidded each other. Glenn always got the last word in. One time, a lady came in with a photo of Liz Taylor, whom Glenn idolized. Glenn thought Liz was the most beautiful woman in the world. The woman said to Glenn, "I want you to make me look like that." Glenn smiled and said, "Lady, you'll need a face-lift first."

The hair in that movie was just nuts—white bouffants and blue upsweeps—and that was just the men! David Lochary's hair looked like some kind of European powdered wig and reminded me of the time a lady preparing to attend the Johnson inaugural ball asked Glenn for a hairdo like Marie Antoinette. It was a high hairdo with curls. Glenn did a wonderful job. She looked magnificent.

When we would make comments on Glenn's customers' hair, he would always say, "I'm the star here, so eat your hearts out!" And there he was, bigger than life up there on the motion picture screen, striking the same pose.

After the movie, the fellows who'd warned me about the film asked what I thought. I told them it was great, and that I had enjoyed seeing my son in it. They looked at me like I was from Mars and began to laugh. They walked us to the car, and I wished them a safe trip home.

Another day I saw Richard reading a copy of *David* magazine. I didn't know at the time that it was a gay publication. I noticed the picture on the cover, a large lady dressed in a red, white, and blue dress. I thought, *Boy, those eyes look familiar.* Richard noticed me staring at the photo and said it was a fellow named Divine, who was performing at the Copa nightclub in Fort Lauderdale only 30 miles away. (I hadn't told Richard about Glenn yet.) Richard said he would like to take me to the club sometime to see Divine perform, that he was really funny. At that time I wasn't ready to see Glenny perform live, so I said no, but that I might be interested if Divine played the Copa again.

In 1981 Glenn brought his act back to the Copa, and Richard approached me again about going. I answered no, but I asked if he would please do me a favor. I asked Richard if he would give Divine a note from me. I wrote my phone number and address and told Richard to ask Divine to call the number while in town. Richard asked if I knew Divine's parents, but I said no.

Richard did go to the Copa, and he gave Glenn the note. When Glenn read the note, he asked, "Did the lady who gave you this number have black hair?" I had dyed my hair blond, though, so Richard replied, "No, she had blond hair." A few months later, when I finally confessed to Richard that I was Divine's mother, he was shocked.

Glenn did call, and when I heard his voice I cried and he cried. I was so nervous that Harris took the phone and talked to him until I calmed down. Glenn told us that he loved us and missed us and wanted to come back home. He wanted to know if I had black hair, as he remembered me. He also said that he would like to forget the past and that he was sorry for all the pain and worry he had caused us. He said, "Mom, when you took my car and told me to leave, that was the best thing you ever did for me. I miss you two." He said he hadn't called before because he was doing things with his life that he didn't think his Dad and I would appreciate or approve of.

I said, "Glenn, Dad and I would like nothing better than having you home. This is your house. We bought this house because we thought you would like it. Everything we did was for you."

That made him happy. After we had talked for more than an hour, he said he was doing a Halloween show at the Copa that Saturday night, and if I wanted him to, he would come home on Sunday for lunch. "Can I come home?" he asked. "Can we be a family again?"

by Loxton

"Divy always had a family, no matter where he was. Whether it was in Baltimore, New York, Amsterdam, or London, there was always a small group of people with whom he shared closeness and love."

—Fashion designer and friend, Zandra Rhodes, from a 2001 interview

Family was a priority for both Harris and me. My parents were born and raised just outside of Zagreb, in Yugoslavia. My father's family, the Vukovich clan, herded sheep, taking care of flocks belonging to many families in the surrounding area. My mother's family, the Smerzerliches, raised sheep. The two families arranged the marriage of 18-year-old Novak and 14-year-old Kathryn, and in 1891, when my mother was just 15 years old, their first child, Donald, was born.

Later that year, mother and father emigrated to the U.S. The trip over was a nightmare—almost no food, few blankets, and terrible overcrowding. On the boat, their beloved Donald, just 7 months old, became ill, died, and was buried at sea.

When they got to America, they settled on a small farm in the tiny western Pennsylvania town of Grindstone. It was a very poor coal-mining town with about 500 houses, a company store—most families were in debt to the company for all of their working lives—a post office, and two churches, one Catholic and one Baptist.

My parents had a four-bedroom house where most of their 15 children were raised. My father worked as a coal miner, and my brothers joined him as soon as they were teenagers. In 1920, when my mother was pregnant with me, my brother Melvin, just 21 years old, was burned to death in a coke oven at the coal mine.

On the farm, we had 10 pigs, a chicken coop, and a milk cow. The women and younger boys worked the farm—milking cows, picking corn, making our own cheese and butter. We even had a smoke shanty, where we cured meat to last through the long and harsh winters.

My father was out of work during the terrible and violent coal miners' strike in 1922, and our family struggled through crippling poverty then and during the Depression. We had to go on relief, and without it we never would have survived. As I write this, only two of us 15 children are still living.

My late husband Harris came from a family of seven in Towson, Maryland just

Our 10th wedding anniversary, 1948

8

north of Baltimore. His dad was a plumber who worked for the Baltimore City Water Department.

When I was 16, my brother Johnny was stationed at Fort Meade in Baltimore. When he got engaged to a local girl, Annabel Klein, he came out to Grindstone to take me, my brother, and my mother to the wedding. While in town for the wedding, I became good friends with Annabel's sister, Bertha,

and instead of going home to Pennsylvania, I stayed in Baltimore and got a job at the Towson Grill on York Road in Towson.

Harris was one of our regular customers at the Grill. He worked the four-to-midnight shift at the Black and Decker plant nearby, and would come in after work and order an Arrow beer and a Western egg sandwich. Harris was tall and handsome, with beautiful eyes, and it got so we'd look forward to see-

ing each other every night around midnight.

We got married in 1938, when I was 18 years old, and we moved into a tiny one-bedroom apartment in Towson, just a few blocks away from the Grill. In 1939 Harris quit his job at Black and Decker and went to work at the American can factory, but in 1940 he went back to Black and Decker and got me a job there as well.

Harris had been designated 4-F by the local draft board because of mobility problems in his arm, so he didn't fight in the war. We later discovered this was the first sign of the muscular dystrophy that confined him to a wheelchair for the last years of his life.

During the war years we both had good jobs, and times were good for us. We wanted to start a family with whom we could share our blessings. In 1940 we were delighted to find out that I was expecting. We worked hard to ready our little third-floor apartment. But one icy winter day, I fell down the steps and lost the baby. We were devastated. As soon as we could, though, we tried again. We lost a second baby in 1943 and worried we might never have a child to share our love with.

In 1944 I started selling war bonds to the people at Black and Decker. I was an aggressive salesperson. People liked me and thought I was a real go-getter. It turned out that I sold the most bonds of anyone in our area. As a prize, I won two tickets to the Army-Navy football game in Philadelphia. At the game, I started to feel funny, and when I went

to the doctor the next week, we discovered that I was pregnant again. Our lives—and the lives of and many, many others—were soon to change forever.

Thursday, October 18, 1945, was a beautiful fall day. The doctor had told me I would give birth around the 19th. I decided to go to my mother-in-law's house so I wouldn't be alone if I went into labor. Harris dropped me off there on his way to work. Mom and I prepared dinner, and we talked and laughed about my having the baby. I was always the happy mother-to-be. We had waited seven years for this to happen, so it was very exciting for all of us.

After we ate, we cleaned up the kitchen, and I thought I had to go to the bathroom. It turned out that my water had broken. I hollered to Mom to call Harris home from work to take me to the hospital. While she looked for the telephone number, I ran to the phone, picked it up, and yelled, "Harris, it's time!" Mom realized that I hadn't dialed the number and said, "Fran, please stay calm," and proceeded to dial. Then I gave her the doctor's phone number to tell him I was coming to the hospital.

Harris came and picked me up, and we were on our way. When we arrived at Women's Hospital on Broadway, the staff quickly put me in a room. About 30 minutes later, the doctor came in and examined me

Our New Baby

Our new baby
Is named
Harris Glenn
Arrived 10-19-45 Weighing 5 lb 14 oz
Mr. and Mrs. Harris Milstead

and said, "If you don't start to have labor pains soon, we'll have to send you home." That made me nervous so I started to pray: "Dear Lord, let me have my baby so they won't send me home." I was very upset, thinking something might be wrong.

Harris stayed with me for an hour, trying to keep me calm. But I knew he was tired and I asked him to go home, telling him I would be all right.

At 10:00 that night the pains started and I called the nurse. She gave me some juice that tasted like grapes. During the night, I just lay there and rubbed my stomach when I felt the pains coming on. I had made up my mind that I wasn't going to bother anybody.

At 7:00 the next morning, the day shift nurse came in, and I told her I was having contractions every five minutes. She timed the pains, and then I was wheeled into the delivery room. I asked the nurses to call Harris. The doctor came in and had them give me a shot. This was many years before natural

childbirth became popular. I guess the last thing the doctor thought he needed to deal with was a crazy Serbian in labor.

When I came to, I saw Harris. The doctor told us we had a beautiful, healthy baby boy. The nurse let us hold him for a while; he had black hair and beautiful blue eyes. I said to the nurse, "He is a little angel given to us by the Good Lord." He was 19 inches long and weighed 5 pounds 14 ounces. We named him Harris Glenn after his father and uncle, and we decided to call him Glenn. He was my pride and joy.

The second day at the hospital, the nurses brought me a booklet on how to care for a baby. On one page, there was a picture of a black crow. Underneath the picture was this line: "Even though your voice may sound crow-like, it's always a lullaby to the baby's ear." I cracked up. I laughed so loud that the nurse heard and asked me what was so funny in that book. I told her I could never carry a tune and that my mother-in-law had always said to me she'd feel sorry for the baby who'd have to listen to me sing.

The same day, while Harris was looking into the hospital nursery, a big, tall serviceman stood beside him. The man commented on the little thing nestled between two larger babies. Harris told him, "That's my son. I wish he was a little bigger, so I wouldn't be afraid to hold him." A few days later I met that man and said, "Let's compare our babies when they are 10 years old." Little did I know that Glenn would grow so large. He was a healthy baby, and that was all that mattered to me.

After seven days at the hospital—normal then, but an extraordinarily long stay by today's standards—we were ready to take our son home. We decided to stop at Harris's Mom's house first. The family was there waiting for us. There was such excitement, and Glenn was bounced from one lap to another. After an hour's stay, we had to leave for home to meet with the nurse, who showed us how to sterilize the bottles and how to bathe Glenn in the bathinet.

After a grueling first day at home, it was time to put our little one to bed. He had his own bedroom decorated in baby-blue with a white crib adorned with toys. We prayed he would sleep. We put a sign on his bedroom door: DO NOT DISTURB. Harris and I couldn't sleep from worrying about Glenn's 10 o'clock bottle or if he was still breathing. We took turns checking on him.

The next night we decided to put him in a bassinet beside our bed. It looked comfortable, and he didn't look as lost as he did in

his big crib. It turned out to be a disaster, though, because every time Glenn made a noise, even a tiny noise, we jumped up to look at him.

After a couple of nights losing sleep, we decided to put him back in the crib. He looked so little and beautiful lying there. I would pick him up and cuddle him. He was my little doll. He was a good sleeper and only cried when he was hungry.

One day a couple of girls from Black and Decker came to visit. I had just started to bathe Glenn when they arrived. He must have gotten excited when he saw them, and he started to pee. Well, the stream went up in

Grandma Milstead and newborn Glenn

the air and we all started to laugh. After he was washed and dressed, we all played with him. The girls gave him a sterling silver spoon and cup with his initials on them, and a pair of white shoes, which I later had bronzed and put beside his baby picture. I have since donated them to the Wesleyan Cinema Archive in Connecticut, where John Waters's memorabilia is stored. I had saved those shoes for 42 years and have always cherished them.

When Glenn started to crawl, we would turn the radio on so he could listen to the music. He would sit on the floor and sway, trying to keep time with the music. His favorite song was "The Teensy Weensy Spider." He liked eating baby food, and he always ate like he was starved. I can remember how excited we were when he got his first tooth. I saved it when it fell out years later. When he got his first haircut, I told the barber I wanted to save the hair. And when he first said "Dada" and "Mama," I wrote it down in his little baby book.

Glenn was 12 months old when he took his first step—I couldn't wait until Harris came home from work to see him walk. I got Glenn out of bed to show him.

We had Glenn dedicated to the Baptist Church when he was 6 months old. In the Baptist Church, dedication is like christening in the Catholic or other faiths. A person is later baptized as a teenager or young adult. Glenn was good in Church and looked cute in his white outfit. Granddad Milstead had never been baptized, but he took the family to church and Bible class every Sunday. Glenn was a member of the Cradle Roll.

My neighbor, Mrs. Diedrich, always bought Glenn ice cream in the evenings when the Good Humor truck came. He really liked his ice cream. One day I started to take a taste and he let out a yelp so loud the neighbors heard. They hollered, "Give that ice cream back to that child." Glenn didn't like sharing his food.

Glenn's first Christmas came when he was only 2½ months old, so he didn't really know what was going on. The next Christmas, though, was quite memorable. Harris put up a garden of artificial trees and flowers in the living room with a model train going around the trees. Both the big Christmas tree and the little trees were lit with beautiful lights. Glenn's toys were wrapped and put under the Christmas tree. He was so excited and surprised to see the little toys. He went from one to another. We let him play for a while, then decided to feed him his breakfast. He ate really fast so he could go back to play. After a few minutes, he threw up from too much excitement.

One night we visited our friends the Millers to play cards. We left Glenn with their son Marvin in the playroom. Marvin called Glenn "Bumpsy," a combination of "Glenn Milstead" and "Dagwood Bumstead." Suddenly we heard a loud shriek, and we ran in to see what had happened. Marvin had bitten Glenn on the chest, and Glenn was in the corner of the playpen crying. It had started with a fight over one of their toys, so we tried to correct the boys, and we took care of the bite. Everybody survived, but this would not be the last time Glenn refused to fight back when attacked.

We showered Glenn with toys—balls, stuffed animals, crayons, and toy trains and cars. He was never interested in playing with any of the sports-related toys. He loved his stuffed animals, though. His favorite was a teddy bear he named Smokey. When we got a dog, Glenn wanted to name it Smokey too, so we did. Glenn played with his stuffed animals for hours, talking to them and having them talk to each other. He even put on little plays with the animals acting out different roles.

When Glenn was about 5, we bought him a drawing set and easel, and he would spend hours drawing and painting. At first he drew stick moms and dads, stick children, and, his favorite, a stick grandma. Then came a period when he drew almost nothing

but airplanes. He continued to draw throughout his school years: As a young teenager, he drew pictures of flowers and brought them to our nursery school for the children to copy. In high school he entered a drawing contest, submitting a beautiful sketch of a house and shrubbery, and another of an intricately detailed fish. Although he didn't win the contest, his art teacher was very impressed and gave him an A.

When Glenn was 5 or 6 years old, we let

him visit with his Grandmother Milstead in Towson. Glenn and his cousin Doris Ann were playing on the porch when Glenn fell down the steps and cut his chin on a brick. His Grandmother rushed him to Union Memorial Hospital. I had been at work and rushed to the hospital as well. I ran into the examination room just in time to see the doctor pull on Glenn's lower lip, revealing a huge gash that went right down to the bone. (The scar is visible, even under Van Smith's heavy makeup, in several of Glenn's movies.) Seeing bone is the last thing I remember before I fainted onto the floor of the examination room. Now the doctors had *two* Milsteads in for treatment!

When I came to, I was told that Glenn had received six stitches. Fainting made me wonder how I would handle the situation if, God forbid, something happened to one of the children at the nursery. Thankfully, I never had to find out.

We lived in Towson until Glenn was 6 years old, then we moved to Loch Raven Village, where Glenn began school. On his first day, he wore a blue Eton suit. He was built so cute and had pretty legs, and his eyes sparkled. School was within walking distance from our home, and Glenn and Judy, the little girl next door, walked together. Glenn made Judy carry his book bag. I told him he should be carrying hers, but he said, "I'm too tired to do

that." After a few months, the skinny little boy named Alexander, who lived a block away, was carrying Glenn's bag. Glenn was lazy, but he got along well in school and seemed to enjoy it.

That summer we took a vacation to see my mother, who lived in western Pennsylvania. Glenn loved to pick her flowers and put them in a vase for the table, something my siblings and I hadn't ever been allowed to do. Her flowers, she said, were to make the outside look pretty. But she loved Glenn and would let him do anything. One day, she said to me in Serbian that Glenn was more feminine than masculine, but the remark went over my head. I didn't know what she meant. He seemed like a healthy little boy to me.

Glenn also went to the YMCA that summer to learn how to swim. On some weekends we would go to Ocean City, Maryland, and Glenn loved swimming in the ocean and playing on the wonderful beaches. Harris bought Glenn a bike and took him to the schoolyard to learn to ride it. Glenn learned fast, as he did with the roller skates Harris bought for him. I didn't go with them because I was afraid Glenn would hurt himself and I didn't want to get upset.

Many people have remarked over the years that they were surprised to see Glenn swim, bounce on a trampoline, or dance in his movie roles. It is true that

Glenn's first day of school, 1951

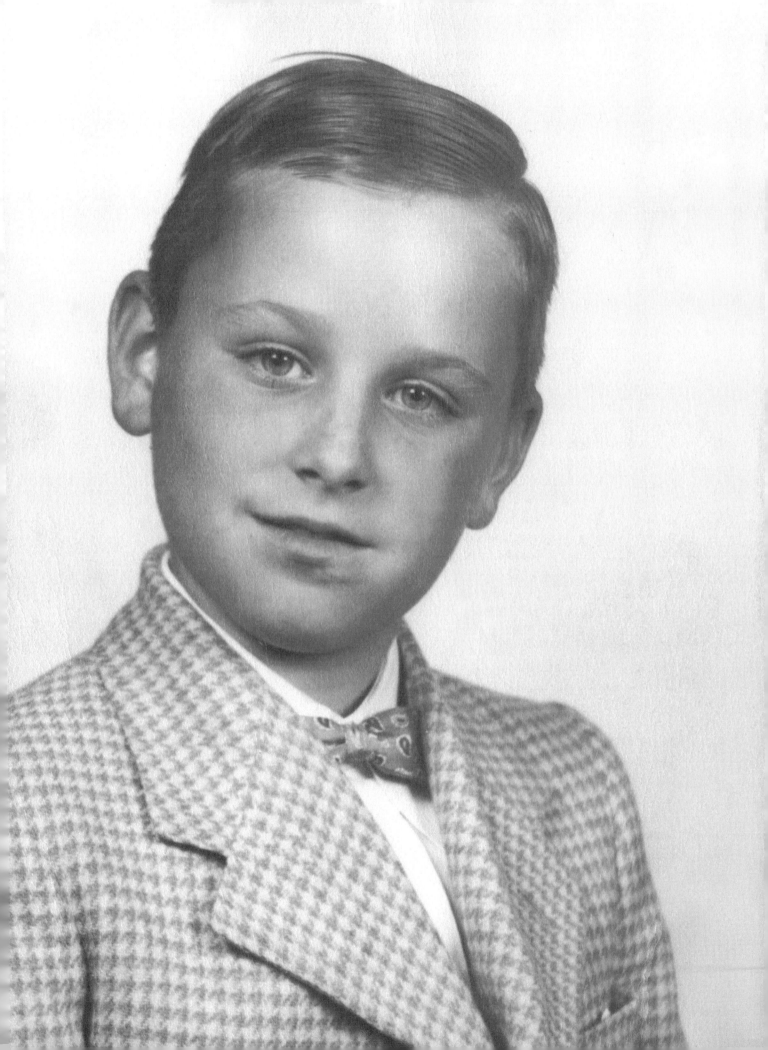

by junior high, when his weight had become a problem, he avoided gym class like the plague. But he was a very active and energetic boy who loved to try new things.

The year after he learned to ride his bike, Glenn decided he wanted to learn to play the piano. We bought him a secondhand piano and promised that if he did well and was really interested in music, we would buy him a new one. To encourage his interest, we signed him up for piano lessons. When we got to the teacher's house for his first lesson, Glenn took one look at her living room and said, "Lady, you'd better clean up your house."

Piano lessons lasted less than a year. Then he wanted to learn to tap-dance. He liked it for a while, and loved doing recitals, but he quit before the first year was up. In his senior year of high school, he wanted to take lessons again, but I refused to pay for them. Usually, though, if Glenn wanted something, and if we could afford it or thought he needed it, we would see that he got it. I guess that stemmed from my own deprived childhood.

In the fourth and fifth grades, Glenn was an average student. He participated in several plays, which he loved to do. He would invite Grandma Milstead to come with us to see him perform. His first role was as a beaver in his school's fall play. I worked several days on his beaver costume, using cotton for his tail and flannel for his fur. Little wires helped his ears stand up. I remember saying to Glenn, "When you get older, you might want to take up acting." He just smiled at me and batted his eyes.

In another of his early roles, he played the emperor Nero. One of my most vivid memories is of my chubby son Glenny dressed in a white robe, as he lay on a bed on the school's stage and ate grapes while two little girls fanned him with leaves taped to tree branches. I think this is how Glenn came to see himself over the years: He loved being the star and having people cater to him. I have been told that *Multiple Maniacs*, which I have never seen, has an almost identical scene—Glenn lying on a divan and being attended to by servants.

Glenn's fifth grade teacher, Mrs. Dalgren, once said to him, "Why don't you take bigger steps when you walk? You

walk just like a girl." It must have upset him, because when he came home he told me about the remark.

Around this time Glenn started to sing in the youth choir at church; he was the alto, and he sang beautifully. His grandmother Milstead had a house in the Baltimore countryside just outside Towson, and we would visit her on weekends. Glenn would sit on a hill away from the house, and we would sit on the porch and listen to him sing. His favorite songs were "Amazing Grace" and "God Bless America." Glenn loved visiting with Grandma Milstead. They would sit for hours and talk about different things and gossip about the family and pick flowers and eat all kinds of goodies.

Glenn also liked to dance. I taught him the two-step and polka. He taught me the Mashed Potato and the Dirty Boogie. He was very light on his feet, even though he was a chubby rascal.

The summer after fifth grade, when Glenn was 11, we took him on a tour of Florida. We did a lot of sight-seeing—anything historical or pertaining to school or art. Glenn loved looking at the old buildings; almost anything visual captured his imagination. In West Palm Beach, we visited my niece Martha, who had three children. She took us to the Parrot, Monkey Jungle, and Lion Country Safari. I can still see Glenn in the Monkey Jungle, a sort of petting zoo, standing with a monkey on each shoulder, smiling from ear to ear. Then we toured Fort Lauderdale, visited

SeaWorld, and went south to Key West. Glenn loved the water show at SeaWorld with beautiful young girls straddling trained dolphins as if they were riding ponies.

We also took Glenn to Quebec for a vacation with Grandpa and Grandma Milstead. We took tours around Quebec, Montreal, and Ontario—making sure to visit any place that seemed educational. We all enjoyed the trip, and Glenn got plenty to eat. Whenever he saw an Italian restaurant, he would say, "It's time to eat!" Spaghetti was his great weakness. Friends of his, after his passing, have told me he could never say no to spaghetti. Glenn always enjoyed spending time with us—until he got to high school and disappeared into the company of his friends.

In sixth grade Glenn hated gym class. This may have been when some of the other boys started to pick on him, but I never heard anything about that until the following year, when he began attending junior high school. So I was very surprised to find out one day that he had come up with a way to hide from the teacher while the class ran laps. The running track was surrounded by trees. Glenn would start running with the other boys, and when the teacher was not looking, he would duck behind one of the trees and wait for the pack to circle the track. Then he'd join them for a few yards before ducking behind another tree. As would happen with many of his deceptive games over the years, he was eventually caught. He told the teacher that he couldn't run with the rest of the boys because he was out of breath.

The teacher told me about this incident, and after we discussed it, I decided to take Glenn to the doctor for a physical examination and to check on a cold he couldn't seem to shake. After examining Glenn, the doctor asked if he could speak to me in his office.

"Is everything all right, doctor? Is Glenn sick?"

"He just has a cold. It's been going around. I'm sure he picked it up in school. But I'd like to ask you a couple of questions about Glenn and his friends, if you don't mind."

I had no idea what was coming next.

"Does Glenn have more little girl friends, or does he play with boys?"

I realized at that point that yes, most of his friends were girls. I told the doctor this.

"What kind of games do they play?" he asked. "Have you watched them?"

Suddenly, I knew what we were talking about. I remembered what my mother had said, and that my niece Anna Marie had once told me that every time she and Glenn played house, Glenn wanted to be the mother. I had laughed at how silly that seemed, thinking little of it.

After hearing about this, the doctor said, "Knowing your son and watching him grow up, I notice that in his body type, his voice, and his mannerisms, he seems to have more feminine traits than masculine ones. I think that that may be the source of his problems at school."

Dining at Jack Dempsey's Restaurant in New York City, 1955

The doctor continued to speak, but I didn't hear anything else that he said. It seemed like he was at the far end of a long, long tunnel. Finally, he gave me a prescription for the cold. But I had one more question.

"Doctor, what can we do about this? What does this mean?"

"I've seen this before, Mrs. Milstead. It seems that some people are just born this way. I really don't know if anything can be done to change a boy like Glenn."

My head spun. Glenn was my baby, and I loved him more than anything in the world, but what would that world do to a person so different? How could I protect him?

In the car, I cried all the way home. Glenn asked me why, and I told him what my mother had said so many years before—that Glenn seemed more like a little girl than a little boy.

He was quiet for a few minutes, and we both pretended to listen to the car radio. Finally, he said, "Mom, will you and Dad stop loving me?"

"No, Glenn, I'll love you until the day I die. You're a human being just like everyone else."

That summer Harris and I went into the day nursery and kindergarten business. We moved from Loch Raven Village to La Paix Lane in Towson, Maryland. The nursery was located in the downstairs portion of our new home. The house was large and had once belonged to Scott and Zelda Fitzgerald. Art students from the State Teachers College in Towson (now Towson University) used to sit on our front lawn and sketch the house for their drawing class.

From the back door of the house, Glenn could walk through the woods to Dumbarton Junior High, where he had started that September. Every morning Glenn would get up, and I would fix him breakfast and pack a little metal lunch pail for him to take to school. He always ate a big breakfast, and I'd send him off with a sandwich, a piece of fruit, and a piece of cake or pie. He'd gather his books and duck out the back door. It was a quick walk down the street to where he met the bus. When he came home in the afternoon, he'd make himself a snack, and we'd talk about his day at school. Then one day I got a notice in the mail from Glenn's school. I was worried that something had been wrong in one of Glenn's classes, until I opened the notice—a bill from the cafeteria for $25. Glenn had been eating his lunch from home and then going through the school lunch line for one of the cafeteria meals. This wouldn't be the last time Glenn charged something to us without our permission.

One afternoon I heard the back door close very quietly, and there wasn't the usual bustle in the kitchen that we were used to hearing when Glenny came home. When I walked around the corner to speak to him, he gave a little jump, like I had caught him

doing something. And before I could ask him what was the matter, he turned his back on me and looked out the back window. "What is it, Glenny?" I asked. He didn't say anything. Finally, he turned around, and I saw little red marks all over his cheeks and above one eye. "What happened?"

"Nothing, Mom," he said as he looked at the floor.

I walked right up to him and tilted his head up so I could look at his face. "You can tell me, Glenn. What happened?"

"It was the ninth graders. They were shooting spitballs at me on the bus."

"What did the bus driver do about this?"

"Nothing, Mom. He just told all of us to sit down, and the other kids just laughed."

The next morning I walked with Glenn to the bus stop and asked the driver what had happened. He told me he didn't remember anything from the day before, and there was not a lot he could do to control the kids while he was driving the bus. He looked over my shoulder at Glenn, who looked down at his shoes. I got up right into the driver's face and said, "You listen to me. If you value your job, you had better learn to control the children, or I will report you to the school authorities." Suddenly, I had his attention. For the rest of the conversation, the driver addressed me as "ma'am" rather than "lady," and Glenn never had any more problems on the bus.

Around this time, Glenn decided to join the Calvary Baptist Church, and he and his Dad were baptized the same Sunday. The pastor, Dr. Day, gave Glenn a Bible. Glenn liked to read it and soon knew every story backward and forward. Two of his favorites were the story of Samson and the story of Daniel in the lion's den. I remember him coming home from Sunday school one afternoon and telling us how awful it was that Samson, this strong man who loved God, had his hair cut off and lost his strength: "Who would cut off all of someone's beautiful long hair?" Glenn wanted to know.

Although Calvary was affiliated with the Southern Baptist Convention, Dr. Day and later his replacement, Rev. Higgenbotham, weren't obsessed with keeping the young people from dancing or going to the movies, and they were very supportive of our letting Glenn make up his own mind about what he wanted to do with his time. Later, when Glenn was having problems in high school and afterward, Rev. Higgenbotham urged me to be patient and to listen to Glenn's side of the story.

At times, the house at La Paix seemed to have a personality of its own. We used to have our friends the Thompsons and the Millers over to visit, and Glenny became very close with Leann Thompson and Rosalind Miller, daughters of our friends who were around Glenn's age. Leann remembers, "The house was old and huge and had lots of crawl spaces, narrow hallways, and closets with little nooks and crannies. Glenn, Rosalind, and I used to crawl all over the house and explore. Glenn would get us into

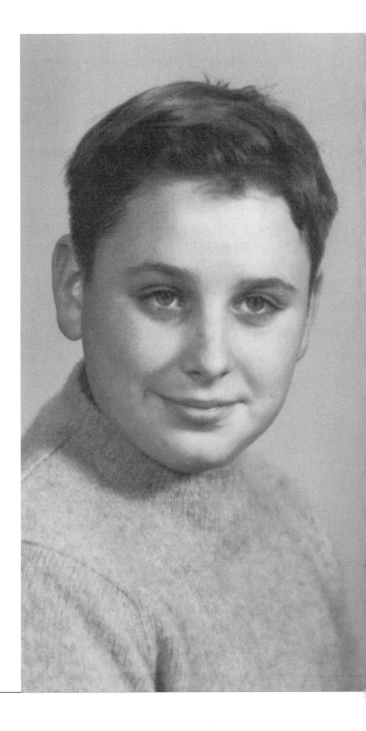

a narrow, dark attic space and then tell us, sitting perfectly still in the total dark, that there were bats in the room and to not make any noise, or they would land on us and bite our ears. Other times he would tell us that the ghosts of the people who used to live there visited him in his room at night and would meet us in a particular room if it was quiet and dark enough."

Glenn and his little friends weren't the only ones who were scared in that huge old place. It always looked like a haunted house to me too. One night Harris and I were lying in bed, and we heard a thumping in the attic. We heard it again the next night, and almost every night thereafter, although only very late after everyone had gone to bed.

Our friend Tim Sullivan, a police officer, stayed with us one night to investigate. Before bed that night, Harris and Tim spread flour on the floor of the attic to detect the footprints of anyone who might be creeping around up there. In the middle of the night there was a huge thump. Tim and Harris went up to investigate, Harris with a black-jack (where he got such a thing I can't imagine) and Tim with his gun. They never did find anything. Many years later when the house was torn down, dozens of squirrel nests were found. We then figured out that our house had been home to dozens, maybe hundreds, of squirrels.

Glenn was a big help to us with the nursery. He would draw pictures of flowers, animals—anything he thought the children would like to color. He also helped his dad transport the children home in the evenings. And when we had Christmas plays, he would play Santa Claus. In fact, every year Harris and I sent a "Santa Gram" to the class from Western Union that read: "On Christmas Eve I call on everyone who's been good and worked hard in the La Paix Nursery School. STOP. So you can expect a visit from me, and my sleigh is full of wonderful things. STOP. Happy Christmas, Santa Claus. STOP." Then, just before we let out for the Christmas holidays, Glenny would come into the nursery dressed as Santa Claus (in a padded costume, of course, but later the padding was unnecessary), carrying a big bag of presents for the children.

One evening Glenn was late coming home from school, and Harris had to leave without him to take the children home. It was almost dinnertime when I heard him trying to sneak in the back door. I rushed toward the back porch ready to dress him down for making us worry, but I stopped when I saw huge bruises on his face. His lip was swollen, there was blood on the front of his shirt, and he was walking gingerly. I couldn't think of what to say. "What happened, Glenny? Where are your books and your jacket?"

"I think they're back in the woods, Mom."

"Take off your shirt, Glenny."

"No, Mom, I really—"

"Take off your shirt, Glenny."

He unbuttoned his shirt, which was

Glenn dressed as Santa

I asked Glenn later why he hadn't hit back. His answer was "In

smudged with dirt and clay, and I saw bruises forming all over his chest and back. I wanted to cry.

"Who did this, Glenny?"

"It was the ninth graders, Mom. They followed me into the woods and wouldn't let me out. They kept playing keep-away with my books. I think they threw them down in the woods, but I don't remember. I'm sorry about my jacket, I just don't remember…"

Finally, he started to cry. I held my baby in my arms, and he told me that the older kids had pushed him around and called him "fatso, sissy, and queer," and when he wouldn't fight back, they hit him until he fell on the ground. When they got tired of hitting him, they just left him in the woods.

I couldn't wait until Harris came home to tell him. I didn't know what to do, but I was getting angrier by the minute. In the meantime, our friend Tim Sullivan, the police officer, came in to pick up his daughter from the nursery. I told him what had happened. He got so angry that he decided to accompany Harris and Glenn to school the next day to talk to the principal. When Harris got home, he, Tim, Glenn, and I talked about the incident. Harris was a quiet, thoughtful, reasonable, and conservative man. I, however, am a Serbian with a hair trigger. Tim and Harris spent half an hour convincing me to stay home the next day while they went to the principal's office because they were concerned I might get violent.

The next day Tim, Harris, and Glenn went to talk to the principal. The boys who beat up Glenn were suspended for a month. One of their mothers called me on the phone that night and asked me why I'd had her son suspended. "Ask your son," I retorted and hung up. Over the years this story has grown into the rumor that Glenn required a police escort every day on his way to school. That was not the case.

I asked Glenn later why he hadn't hit back. His answer was "In Sunday school, Jesus tells us to turn the other cheek."

The day after the incident, Glenn told his teacher that he had lost his homework and needed another copy of the assignment. His teacher tartly replied, "My heart bleeds for you," and she gave him a failing grade. So off to school I went to talk to her.

Before we had moved from Loch Raven to La Paix, Glenn had joined a Boy Scout troop at Loch Raven Catholic Church. Loch Raven was less than three miles from our house on La Paix Lane, so Glenn was able to continue in the Boy Scout troop after we moved. He loved being in the parades, and the exercises were good for him, but he hated the camp.

About six months after the beating incident, the troop had a program at the church during which the scouts were presented with prizes. We waited for Glenn to be called onstage, but he never was. We didn't know what had happened or why he had been overlooked.

At the end of the year, there was anoth-

Sunday school, Jesus tells us to turn the other cheek."

er program. Glenn invited his grandmother and aunt to go see it. He was overlooked again, and he was so embarrassed that he walked out of the auditorium. I went up to the scoutmaster and demanded an explanation. I asked if the problem was that Glenn was the only non-Catholic. The scoutmaster apologized, but Glenn never went back.

One year Glenn had a birthday party. He and his friends had a blast eating hamburgers, hot dogs, and watermelon, and playing games, including a guessing game in a dark room to see if you knew who was kissing whom. Harris and I were amazed at what they came up with. The birthday party was a success: *Everybody* went home with a prize.

Like most of the kids his age, Glenn was in love with music, movies, and television. He would go see anything with Marilyn Monroe or Elizabeth Taylor. By the time he was in high school, of course, he no longer went to the movies with Harris and me. Instead, he would go with his friends. Still, I remember that he was always talking about Marilyn Monroe and Liz Taylor.

When Glenn was a sophomore at Towson High School, *Some Like It Hot* featuring Marilyn Monroe was playing at the local theater, and it quickly became one of his favorite films. The movie is about two musicians, played by Tony Curtis and Jack Lemmon, who hide out with an all-girl band after they witness a gangland shooting. To fit in, they have to wear women's clothes, and Jack Lemmon has to fight off the marriage proposal of a lonely retired widower. It wasn't until after Glenn passed away that some of his fans pointed out to me what an impact this movie may have had on him.

Glenn loved Elizabeth Taylor even more than Marilyn. He would go see anything she was in, and he thought she was the most beautiful woman in the world. When Glenn was a teenager, some of her most famous movies were first released, and he went to see every one: *Cat on a Hot Tin Roof* when he was a freshman, *Suddenly, Last Summer* when he was a sophomore, *Butterfield 8* when he was a junior, and *Cleopatra* right around graduation time. Glenn's high school sweetheart, Diana Evans, tells me that they went to see *Cleopatra* almost a dozen times, and that Glenn always cried during the death scene at the end of the movie.

Many of Glenn's fans have commented on how much these same movies meant to them while growing up. Nowadays it is wonderful to see Elizabeth Taylor showing appreciation and love for her fans through her charity work for the American Foundation for AIDS Research and similar causes.

Harris and I bought Glenn his own TV and record player, which he kept in his room. Harris and I didn't really pay much attention to the music he liked, but over the last few years, I have come to recognize

from the radio, television, movies, and advertising many of the songs that Glenn used to sing along with: "Jim Dandy" by LaVern Baker, "I Only Have Eyes for You" by the Flamingos, "Save the Last Dance for Me" by the Drifters, and "There's a Moon Out Tonight" by the Capris, just to name a few. Glenn loved music, especially music by many of the black singers who at that time were just starting to make a lot of records and be heard frequently on the radio. Every day Glenn would rush home from school and run up to his bedroom to hear and watch the latest dance hits on Baltimore's TV dance program, *The Buddy Deane Show*.

John Waters was about Glenn's age and shared many of his interests, even though the two did not meet until later. According to John, "Dick Clark's *American Bandstand* was everywhere else in the country, and the more regular kids that danced on the show every day were nationally famous. We never

Glenn's birthday

saw Dick Clark in Baltimore. We had *The Buddy Deane Show* where the kids had higher hair, wore more eye makeup, had more extreme clothes. It was just pushed one step further than *American Bandstand.*

"In my neighborhood, the girls had big bullet hairdos and stuff, but it wasn't really cool among my friends to be on *The Buddy Deane Show.* But everyone watched it if just to make fun of it. I loved it. I made fun of it, but watched it every day."

John would go on to make *Hairspray,* his homage to *The Buddy Deane Show* and the last film starring Glenn.

In 1960 while Glenn was a sophomore at Towson High, we moved from La Paix Lane to our new home at 1425 Francke Avenue in Lutherville, Maryland, another suburb of Baltimore. We had an apartment upstairs and the day nursery downstairs. Glenn became friends with one of the neighborhood girls, Carol Wernig, who lived across the street. I thought she was a little too fast for Glenn to be associating with, and I spoke with her stepmother who said, yes, Carol was having some problems in school. Harris and I tried to keep Glenn from spending time with Carol, but he wouldn't listen. Eventually, Carol introduced Glenn to a circle of people who changed his and our lives forever.

Carol still laughs when she thinks back on those years. "Lutherville is kind of a button-down shirt, tweedy neighborhood," she says. "Divine lived right across the street, and my father had worked with one or both of his parents at Black and Decker. Glenn and I were both kind of outcasts. I was a little outrageous for the neighborhood, and Glenn was heavy and didn't have a lot of friends, and we just kind of gravitated to one another. I spent my junior and senior year of high school grounded. The only way I could get out of the house was if I went out with Glenn. My parents trusted Glenn. So we would take turns driving to school. And on the days when I drove, I would drop Glenn off and pick my friends up, and we would cut school, and then I would invariably forget to go back and pick him up, which didn't endear me to him. But we had that kind of relationship—a little one-sided.

"I met John Waters, who lived about two blocks from us, since I was continually grounded. My job was to rake the leaves in our yard, and John kind of just wandered by one day while I was out raking the leaves. I think he was attracted to my hair, which was green at the time, and it matched this acne medication I used called Queen Helene Mint Julep mask, which was something Glenn also loved. We used to play poker on Saturday nights for my pimple cream. I introduced Glenn and John, and then I introduced David Lochary to John as well."

At this time, Glenn was particular about his appearance, even though he was heavy.

By his second year in high school, he had developed expensive taste in clothes; he loved nice slacks and well-tailored sports jackets. Our late-summer trips to the clothing store to buy his fall wardrobe got more and more expensive every year.

Many of the most stylish clothes, though, were only available in sizes for thinner young men. So I took Glenn to Dr. Singer, who was a diet specialist. Glenn weighed in at 185 pounds and said he wanted to weigh 145 by graduation. Dr. Singer put him on diet pills, and Glenn began to watch what he ate. This was 1961, and we trusted the doctor completely. No one had any idea how dangerous and addictive amphetamine diet pills could be. The medication was widely prescribed, and Glenn never seemed to experience any side effects.

One of the things that cracked me up in the movie *Hairspray* was how Glenn's character Edna and even her daughter Tracy were taking "appetite suppressants on doctor's orders," and that Edna would often glare at her husband and daughter, complaining, "My diet pill is wearing off!"

As a senior, Glenn really started to slim down, and he began to look handsome. He attended to his diet and went to the doctor faithfully every Wednesday night. He was proud of himself, and everyone complimented him. We had a mirror in the front hallway of our apartment, and I can remember Glenn standing in the front room pretending to do something else—like listen to me—while taking quick glances at himself in the mirror and smiling. Glenn said Hamberger's Store had a red sports jacket in the window that he would like to buy. I told him that when he lost the weight I would be happy to buy it for him.

But Glenn still liked his food. He even started to cook things for himself. He loved spaghetti and roast beef, but when he began to diet in high school, he ate almost nothing but steaks and salads. I would go to the butcher shop and have them cut hind quarters, which I would put in individual servings in the freezer. Then Glenny would fix his own dinner when he got home from school. I can remember coming upstairs from the day nursery to the delicious smell of garlic. I would walk into the kitchen and find Glenny cooking his steak, with the salad already prepared and on the kitchen table. Never—and I mean never—did he offer me even a single bite of his food no matter how much I praised his cooking!

Glenn's high school sweetheart was Diana Evans, the daughter of one of my friends. I thought he needed a date and fixed them up. Diana still thinks fondly of him. "He was a lovely young man. He was 13, and I was 14. This was in 1958. His mother decided that he needed a date, and I was the candidate. I met him at the door with my grandmother, and he brought me a box of Marzipan candy, which was his favorite, and we proceeded to go to this dance. His cousin, Ann-Marie, was our chauffeur, or

PHOTOS COURTESY OF DIANA EVANS.

chauffeuse, I guess, because he wasn't old enough to drive. They played songs like "At the Hop" by Danny and the Juniors, "Rockin' Robin" by Bobby Day, and "Who Wrote the Book of Love?" by the Monotones. Even though Glenn was a huge music fan, neither one of us could dance. It was kind of funny, so we spent the evening talking to each other, just kind of alien. He was not used to girls, and I was not used to boys. Actually, I beat boys up. So it was initially a very tedious kind of situation. Still, he was such a sweetheart that we had a lovely time, and after that we proceeded to date for maybe six or seven years.

"We went to many proms together: his junior and senior, and my senior prom. We attended every dance, and because Glenn was such a perfectionist, each and every time we had to look perfect. He spent months trying to lose weight before each dance. We had a great time after we learned to dance. His mother taught us how to cha-cha, and after that we really took off. Glenn learned all of the dance steps from *The Buddy Deane Show* on TV, all the ones that John put in *Hairspray*: the Bird, the Mashed Potato, the Dirty Boogie, and of course, the Madison."

"I can do all those dances still," recalls John Waters, "not that I'm going to, and I wouldn't in public. I think the Madison…is the only dance I'll ever do in public. I do that when I go to the reunions on *The Buddy*

Glenn and Diana's first date in 1958, and Diana's high school prom—hair by Glenn

Deane Show. It's still a great, great dance, and me, Mary Vivian Pearce, Divine, and the others used to all do it drunkenly after the bars in my apartment. You know, put the Madison on and I would teach people how to do it years before *Hairspray.*

"Don't forget that this was before the real '60s began. That was a weird time. It was before the Beatles, and it was before hippies, but it was after Elvis, and it was this weird time when the fashions were the most insane. Those giant beehive hairdos were not the rebel look. That was how your mother looked too. In certain neighborhoods in Baltimore they had mother-daughter look-alikes. That wasn't the way to rebel. The way to rebel was to have straight, ironed hair. So it was a very confusing time for fashion in Baltimore. As I've said before, Baltimore is truly the hairdo capital of the world. During the '60s, even if you were 13 years old you went to the beauty parlor twice a week and had these bullet hairdos."

Diana remembers, "Glenny and I did everything together when there was a chance. We were both going to school, so we had weekends and that was about it. But as far as I'm concerned, I was his high school sweetheart. I have his ring; we're still actually going steady!

"I think that Glenny was very artistic from the very beginning of his life. He loved things to be lovely, perfect. He loved working with fashion. He took his part-time job at the florist shop very seriously and would con-stantly bring me lovely bouquets and flowers, yellow orchids—whatever he could think of. Each and every dance we went to was a wonderful new creation. My hair never looked as good as it did when we were going out. He always took care of my hair. He would cut it and tell me how to wear it, and he was just very artistic. And he had a good eye for fashion. I think that one of the reasons he wanted everything to be perfect each time we went out was that he had suffered so much harassment at his high school that, at this point, having lost weight and having a girlfriend to go to dances with, he was trying his best to be everything he thought people wanted him to be."

Around this time, Glenn started doing my hair as well. I would get up early in the morning on a Saturday and put on the cof-fee, and Glenn would come in for breakfast still dressed in his bathrobe. After we ate, he would sit me down in a kitchen chair and start in on my hair.

His was the most gentle, soft touch I have ever known—except when he was doing my hair. He was determined to wrench my Yugoslavian hair into the perfect bouffant, and no yelps of pain from me or anybody else were going to get in his way.

Before some of the chemical processors that they have now, you had to use what was called the fingers-and-comb method, which took between one and two hours. First, you washed the hair, which Glenn would do for me in the kitchen sink. Then you applied the

setting gel and put the hair in rollers. You dried the hair under the dryer, took the rollers out, and brushed and teased the hair to get it as high as possible. Finally, the hair was shaped and blasted with a huge amount of hairspray. Glenn could get my hair higher and more beautifully shaped than any professional hairdresser I ever went to.

Glenn was also very creative in decorating around the house. I would bring home a flower arrangement from the florist or do one myself as part of holiday decoration, and he would come in behind me and redo it, always making it look better.

Everybody who knew Glenn knew that he loved Christmas. He would spend hours decorating the Christmas tree—it had to be real. If we had bought an artificial one, he would have disowned us. I remember one year he frosted the tree completely white and put beautiful blue balls on it. It rotated on an electric base, and on the other side of the room he had put a wreath, also frosted white, with red ornaments.

There is a picture of me from one of these holiday seasons standing with one of my friends in the living room. Glenn had just done my hair that morning, and you can see a small Christmas tree he'd decorated in the background. In the picture, my hair and the Christmas tree are just about the same shape!

When Glenn was 16, Harris and I bought him a car. One of my friends once told me that children learn to walk when they are 1 year old and lose the ability at 16. This was the way it was with Glenn. I

remember his first day driving the car to school. He came home in the late afternoon, and I smelled tobacco on him. I asked Glenn if he had been smoking with his friends. He batted his eyes and denied it.

It seemed like Glenn changed overnight. He had his car and a lot of friends, whom he never brought around when Harris and I were home. And we told him not to let other kids drive his car, but he did. Then he would lie to us about it. I always told him, "It's easier to remember the truth," but he never took it to heart. I told him that Abraham Lincoln had said that no man had a good enough memory to be a successful liar.

Near the end of Glenn's senior year in high school, Calvary Baptist Church had its annual Senior Sunday to honor the young men and women who were about to graduate. Glenn was scheduled to give part of the sermon, and he had prepared a lovely little talk. Of course, he was very proud of how handsome he looked as a thin young man, and he was delighted to be able to wear the red sports jacket that we had finally bought him at Hamberger's.

He disappeared into the rear of the church at the beginning of the service, and Harris and I waited for him to take the lectern. Finally, it was Glenn's turn to speak, and we were shocked to see his beautiful red jacket replaced by a drab gray sport coat that hung off his body and bulged at the shoulders. He gave a wonderful talk about how some young folks were natural leaders

and that other young men and women were followers and that each person had a part to play in their church and community in the Lord's plan. But I couldn't take my eyes off that big gray coat.

After the service, he met us outside the church, wearing his red jacket again. I asked, "Glenny, what happened to your coat when it was time for you to speak?"

"Oh, Mom," he said in an embarrassed voice, "Reverend Higgenbotham told me it was too loud, and he made me wear his jacket instead!"

Little did I know that the red sports jacket was nothing compared to some of Glenn's other clothes.

CHAPTER 3

"You can't find anything my size, like this, on the rack.
Women my size just don't wear these sorts of things."

—Divine in a 1972 interview from the documentary film *Divine Trash* (1998)

After high school graduation, Glenn decided to take a course in cosmetology at the Marnilla Beauty School. He told us he would start in the summer and if the he didn't like it, he would go to the Alfred Institute and study to be a florist. He enrolled at the Marnilla Beauty School in May 1963. He continued to set my hair on weekends, and I always got compliments. Once he did my hair so high before a wedding I attended that I was criticized for taking attention away from the bride! He did very well, and the instructors said I should send him to New York to a styling school. But Glenn didn't want to go and decided to stay and get his hairdresser's license in Baltimore.

After he graduated, I went with him to David and Martin's Beauty Salon, considered to be the best in Towson at that time. The lady who ran the salon had a niece in our nursery, and I thought this would be a good way to help Glenn get a job. She asked him to do the receptionist's hair as an audition. After they saw his work, they hired him. He worked there for a while, partied with the owners, and started to stay out late

at night. He was always rushing to go to work the next morning.

Carol Wernig remembers this wild time. "Just after high school, I discovered that Glenn liked to dress in drag, long before anybody knew what drag was. And the way he would get away with it was that he would rent one of the bars in Towson and have big costume parties. We would all come in costume, and Glenn would come in drag. He would have these parties as frequently as he could finance them. He was into the homosexual and drag scene before I think even he knew what it was—certainly before anybody who had been to Towson Senior High knew what it was!"

"In the summer of 1963," says Diana Evans, "Glenn was attending cosmetology school, and right around that time, he met David Lochary, future leading man of John Waters's movies. David was just about the most important person that Glenn ever met: David was always telling Glenn to do whatever he wanted and to be whoever he was. Whatever Glenn was saying that he wanted to do, David was always encouraging him.

Diana with Glenn dressed as Elizabeth Taylor, Halloween 1963

"Glenn began wearing female clothing at this time as part of a lot

As a matter of fact, it was right after Glenn met David that he threw the Halloween party where he went dressed as Elizabeth Taylor.

"People always said that Divine, who will always be Glenny to me, was an actor, not a drag queen, and I think this is totally accurate: Glenn began wearing female clothing at this time as part of a lot of anger and rebellion on his part. He was out of school, working, and under no one's thumb, and he seemed to be saying to all of those people who had harassed him for so long, 'OK, if this is what you think I am, then here it is.' Believe me, Glenn never enjoyed wearing women's clothes. In fact, the time that we dressed him as Elizabeth Taylor, he looked down at me from his perch on high-heel shoes and said, 'This is the most uncomfortable thing I have ever done. How do women do this all the time?'"

"Try to remember," points out Glenn's pastor Leland Higgenbotham, "that those were the days before even civil rights, much less gay rights or women's rights or any of the consciousness-raising movements of our times. It may be difficult for many to imagine what our society was like, really. So many changes have taken place. His mother recalls the time I made Glenn wear my jacket instead of the red one he had brought. It was not long before Glenn began to show up in all sorts of amazing hairdos and dress. It became a great concern to his parents and me. We had no idea what was going on. As their Pastor, I felt totally inadequate."

Diana says, "Glenn never showed any tendency toward going in the drag direction or any kind of tendency other than being I guess what you'd call a 'pure boy' to me. I remember that I was compared to Elizabeth Taylor many times. We had many disagreements about her. He would say to me, 'You know, your skin texture is different than Elizabeth's, and your eyes aren't the same color, but I think if we fixed your hair you would look a little bit more like her.' When we started going out on double dates to dances and things, I noticed a definite tendency to try to steer me in the Elizabeth Taylor direction.

"But this time, *he* went to the party as Elizabeth Taylor and looked wonderful. I still think that a lot of this was at David Lochary's insistence.

"My mom was really surprised when David and Glenn showed up at our house the night of the party and the hair and makeup turned into a big production between Glenn and David with my Mom and me feeling totally excluded. This was the first time I'd seen anything like that in Glenn. Of course, he had gone to hairdresser school and that has a connotation that goes with it, but it didn't strike me. All of a sudden, though, he did have a tendency to pick out shoes and have them dyed to match dresses. And he really got into hairdos and makeup. He used to chase me around, trying to put makeup on me!

"At this time, *gay* didn't mean a thing to me. Still, to this day I couldn't identify a gay

f anger and rebellion on his part."

person to you right off the street. He was an artistic young man, he was talented. Just because he wasn't hairy and didn't do a bunch of guy stuff like grunt or make car noises, I had no concept of his being gay or anything like that. He was a thoughtful young man to me, treated me as if I were a princess, and to this day no one ever quite comes up to his standards. I was his girl; he did everything he could to help make me happy, and I just enjoyed it."

After Glenn's death, I was visiting with Diana, and she showed me a picture and asked who I thought it was. My response was, "Is that Elizabeth Taylor?" It wasn't. It was a picture of Glenn from that Halloween party.

When I asked Channing Wilroy, Glenn's friend and fellow actor from *Pink Flamingos* (1972) what his first impression of Glenn was, he let out a low laugh that could have come from Vincent Price. "I just went to his parties at first, the ones where he would rent out a bar in Towson and hold court in drag. This was the same time that I met John Waters through Pat Moran, so the whole group was starting to come together around that time. To me he was just another tall, swishy, slightly chubby drag queen. You know, the Liz Taylor period. He was always very good at it, but of course when his makeup man Van Smith came along later, things got even better. His weight was really going up and down during this period. He was constantly dieting and taking diet pills. It was like, 'This week, I'm 200 pounds, the next

week, I'm 130.'

"We used to go over to Washington, 40 miles down the road, a lot. This was the early '60s, and they used to have drag balls over there, and Glenn loved to go. They would have beauty contests, and he would always do very well. Of course, he wasn't the brash, loud Divine at this point. He was very demure and sexy, and he would walk like Jayne Mansfield: dragging feather boas, slinking along—that kind of look. Much thinner than he turned out later but still *zaftig*—make sure that word gets in your book.

"There was one time we almost got killed at one of these balls. Glenn was going to win [first prize at] the ball—he and his feather boa was a pretty hard act to follow—and one of the other drag queen's boyfriends was there and started a fight. All of a sudden, there were all of these knives out all over the place, and everybody ran for the door. But the door opened into the room and there was this huge crush of people against it, which of course meant the door would not budge. So then all of those people turned around and started to brandish knives. A couple of the guys got hurt really badly, but Glenn found a way to stay out of the fray."

People have asked me over the years about Glenn's high school years and after, and they seem surprised when I tell them he

wore stylish sport coats and nicely pressed slacks. The only times Glenn ever dressed in costumes that I knew about were Halloween, New Year's, and high school plays. In the last years of his life, of course, I knew what his "work clothes" were (this is what he always called them), and I enjoyed seeing him in some of his movie appearances. But it is important to remember that whenever he appeared on television to be interviewed, he wore very elegant designer suits, usually with a stylish bow tie. It was the same with his younger days

One evening, while Glenn was still living at home, Harris and I had gone out. We came home unexpectedly early. We saw a few cars at our house, and when we came into the front door, his company was running out the back door. The living room smelled funny to me, like they'd been smoking pot. But Glenn denied it. I asked, "Why did they all leave? Are you ashamed of us or ashamed of your friends?" He said he was afraid we would get angry and say something to them.

After working for a while, Glenn decided he needed a new car. Harris and I went with him to the Buick dealership. He picked out a beautiful new black and white Skylark convertible. He promised he would make the monthly payments, but he needed a down payment. His Dad helped him with it, and we made him promise us that he wouldn't let anyone else drive the car. One morning, I decided to surprise him by washing and waxing his car for him. After finishing the outside of the car, I started to clean the inside, and I found 14 unpaid parking tickets in the glove compartment.

When Glenn woke up, we discussed the car and the tickets with him. He just thought he should be able to park wherever he pleased. On Monday, his day off, we took him to the police station to pay the tickets. I thought they would give him a fine for late payments, but they just thanked him and patted him on the back.

A couple of months later, I received a call from Reverend Higgenbotham at our church telling me to ask Glenn to remove his car from the church parking lot and move it to Mario and Richard's beauty shop, which

is where Glenn was working at that time. I called Glenn at work, and he said he was busy and couldn't get away, and he asked if I would move it for him. Harris took me to the church and dropped me off by Glenn's car. I looked inside and saw the F-word scribbled in black crayon on the white leather front seats. I took the car to a garage to have the word scrubbed off because I couldn't do it. And I was ashamed to face the preacher the following Sunday.

Another time, my friend Dolly had to go downtown. As we were driving down Howard Street, she noticed a Skylark convertible just like Glenn's in front of us. "Hey, look," said Dolly. "That guy has a car just like Glenn's." We moved up behind it and I saw the license plate. It *was* Glenn's car. His friend Barry was driving it, and there was another young man in the front seat.

"Where do they think they're going in my son's car?" I asked. "Get behind them and see where they're going."

Dolly suddenly changed lanes as the Buick went around a corner, and car horns blared all around us. We sped up and got right behind them, and the young man in the passenger seat turned around and looked at us and tapped Barry on the shoulder. Barry looked in the rearview mirror and gunned the engine, changing lanes again. The tires screeched as he took off.

"Keep behind them!" I yelled, and Dolly changed lanes again, cutting off more traffic and bringing more shouts and honking horns our way.

"Frances, I've gotta keep my car in one piece," she snapped, and before I could say anything else, I saw Glenn's Buick disappear around the corner almost a full city block ahead. When we turned to follow it, the car was nowhere in sight.

We gave Glenn hell that night at dinner. "Glenn," I told him, "If your friends are out in your car and have an accident, we could be sued."

His response: "Mom, it's my car and I can lend it to my friends if I want to."

"Glenny, you always do just what you want to do. You only think of yourself and your friends."

He rolled his eyes at me and looked bored. Then he looked down at the pot roast on his plate and dug in, trying to ignore me.

It seemed as if the more upset Harris and I got with Glenn, the more amused he became. When I would "get my Serbian up" and yell at him about a parking ticket or a bounced check, he would dismiss me with a Cleopatra-like wave of his hand and say mysteriously, "I'm a star." This meant nothing to me at the time. I thought he was talking about the beauty shop: His boss loved him and so did the ladies. But I know now that he was dropping little hints about the film work he was doing with John Waters.

After working for almost a year at David and Martin's, the job he had gotten just out of cosmetology school, Glenn decided to go to work at James Stroumbis's beauty salon in Towson. His customers followed him. He had the wives of some of the Orioles and Colts players. They all loved Glenn's work. James and Salvatore, who worked there before moving to Florida, often said they wished they could style hair like Glenn. Salvatore still talks about Glenn working barefoot, something the customers all found hilarious.

"I had been very close friends with Frances and Harris for many years," remembers James Stroumbis. "And I knew Glenn from the time he was 12 or 13 years old. In fact, when Glenn was in high school, my son attended the La Paix Nursery run by his parents. Before he was even in high school, I knew he had been fixing his mother's hair and doing a wonderful job.

"My shop was in the Dulaney Valley Shopping Center on Dulaney Valley Road. It was in one of those strip shopping centers which also had a restaurant, a bank, and a clothes shop. At one point, some of the office space was rented out to Spiro Agnew, who was county executive at the time and running for Maryland governor. He was Greek, and I am Greek, and he used to come in the shop to say hello. I don't remember if he ever met Glenn, though. People laugh when they think about those two in the same shop making small talk.

"Prospect Hill Cemetery is on the hillside next to the shopping center. That's where Glenn is buried now, so he's facing the place where he used to work.

"I have an old flyer we used to circulate to advertise the shop that shows a drawing of a woman with a bullet upsweep. It says: 'For the best in hair fashions, make an appointment with Mr. James, Mr. Salvatore, or Mr. Glenn. Enjoy our pleasant atmosphere with FM music, coffee, or tea, while we do the rest (frosting, coloring, setting of wigs and hairpieces our specialty). We are happy to introduce our new high-fashion hair stylist Mr. Glenn.'

"Glenn specialized in really fancy hairdos, particularly those beehives and upsweeps that were really popular in the

early '60s. It used to take him hours. You know, to make money in the business at the time you had to be fast and turn over a high number of customers, but Glenn was just the opposite. He was a perfectionist. Looking back on it now, I realize we should have charged a lot more money than we did for those haircuts Glenn did. I was doing a customer every 15 minutes, and he was taking about three hours per head! But my hairdos couldn't compare to his. Ladies would come to the shop specifically for him and would wait three or four hours to see him, and his hairdo would take another three hours, so the customer would just be at the shop all day. He used to work barefoot and tell funny stories, and the customers loved him.

"He was always joking around, and his young friends would come by the shop to say hello. I didn't know who they were at the time, but looking back, I now know that they were Mink Stole, David Lochary, and John Waters. Some of them seemed like odd young kids, but they were always very polite.

"One day the store was packed with customers, and the door to the shop opened

"Faggot? What does that mean?" "You know, like Glenn."

and in walked this beautiful, dark-haired woman. I was a virile young man, around 40 at the time, and I would never turn my eyes away from a beautiful woman, no matter how many customers were waiting in line. This one looked like an Italian sexpot: built like anything, high heels, expensive shoes, diamond earrings. I couldn't take my eyes off her. The shop was so quiet, all you could hear was Percy Faith on the FM radio. From behind me, I heard Salvatore say, 'Don't you know who that is, James?'

"'No,' I said. 'Who is that?'

"'That's Glenn, James.'

"So I guess we all knew he was a little bit different, but it didn't bother me. I always liked Glenn, and I loved his parents.

"There was one incident at the shop which I remember, and it hurts me to this day to think about it. It was Glenn's day off, and there was a lady who was a regular customer up at my desk paying for her haircut, and Frances was there, also getting ready to pay. The two ladies didn't know each other. Somebody, maybe a customer— I don't remember—said the word *faggot*. And my English was terrible in those days. I was always missing out on bits of conversation and having to ask about English words and what they meant. So I said, 'Faggot? What does that mean?' The lady turned to me and said, 'You know, like Glenn.' Suddenly I knew what she meant, and before I could say anything, Frances whipped around and said very quietly, 'I'll

have you know I am his mother.' Then she turned and left. I felt just terrible for her."

Glenn's clients loved him, and so did we. But he did try our patience. One year he decorated the house for Christmas. The tree was flocked white and trimmed with magenta teardrops and revolved on a musical stand. I later took a picture and used it to make Christmas cards to send to all my friends and relatives. The floral arrangements he did to match the tree were beautiful, some with candles and ornaments, each one prettier than the last.

I said to Harris, "Isn't it nice of Glenn to do this for us?" Well, we were wrong again. Glenn knew that his Dad and I had planned a trip to Bermuda for New Year's. When we got to Bermuda, Glenn called to see if we had arrived safely. When we arrived home several days later, everything was in order, and Glenn was happy to see us. Two weeks later I received a bill from the Towson Florist for $350, much more than the Christmas flowers had cost. I called the shop, and they told me Glenn had a party while we were away. We talked to Glenn, and he promised he would pay us later because he was short of cash just then. But he forgot about it, of course.

Years later after Glenn's funeral, two of the young women who had helped me at the nursery during these years told me they

"I'll have you know I am his mother."

helped Glenn rearrange the furniture and decorate the house for the party, and that somehow he had convinced them to swear to secrecy. He could be a charming and persuasive fellow, I guess.

Glenn's high jinks weren't all we had to worry about. In 1964 and early 1965, a serial killer was on the loose in Baltimore. One Thursday evening in early December 1964, Glenn told us that he was having a few girls over to the house and was going to make them dinner and practice on their hair because they were supposed to be in a wedding the following week and wanted a certain style. Harris and I went out to dinner and then visited some friends. We arrived home at 11 o'clock and went to bed after watching Johnny Carson on TV. Glenn and his company had left, and the kitchen was clean. We heard Glenn come home and go to bed before we drifted off to sleep. The next morning he got up and went to work. About 9:30, he called me from the beauty shop, told me not to get excited, and explained to me that the police were taking him to the station to be questioned. One of the girls from the night before, Sally Crough, had been murdered during the night. I told Glenn that whatever questions the police asked, please tell the truth. The truth would be easier to remember.

The girls all worked at the Social Security office, and they had a carpool. It had been Sally's turn to drive, and when Sally didn't show up, one of the other girls decided to drive instead. When the others got to work,

they called Sally's house but didn't get an answer. They tried several times, and became concerned. They told the boss that something must have happened to her, and the boss then sent a fellow to Sally's apartment. Sally's door was locked, but the fellow could hear the radio playing, so he went to the landlord and told him. They both went upstairs to her apartment. The landlord opened the door, and they found Sally strangled on the bed. Lamps and furniture were turned over, showing she had put up a struggle. Sally was the killer's 11th victim.

The murder made the headlines, and the police had the five people who had been at Sally's house that night, including Glenn, at the Police Station all day for questioning. Glenn and the others were assured that their names would not be released to the newspaper. Glenn told them that after he had set the girls' hair they all had gone to Sally's and watched TV, drinking Coke and eating potato chips before he and one girl left, leaving a fellow and the other two girls there. The other couple left soon after Glenn. The girls all had rollers in their hair—Sally's rollers were found all over the bedroom—and Glenn was to do the comb-out the next day. We later learned that the murderer had been sitting on the fire escape by the kitchen window and could see them in the living room. The police found his cigarette butts out there.

That Sunday I received a phone call telling me that the newspaper had mentioned Harris as being involved in the murder. I had

to explain that Glenn's first name was also Harris. The people in church all thought it was his Dad. This whole ordeal was a nightmare, and I wouldn't wish it on anyone. Our phones were tapped, and everybody was talking about Glenn and the murder. I thought for sure it would ruin my business.

Reverend Higgenbotham came to our house after the church service to talk and pray with us. His sermon the following Sunday was about how the police could promise you one thing and then do the opposite.

The police asked the kids to attend Sally's funeral and give a signal if they noticed anyone suspicious. They were given tear gas to carry with them, and they were told to tell their parents where they were going at all times.

The following month the killer was captured between Baltimore and Washington. The man was married and had two children and a pregnant wife. He was later committed to a mental hospital. People have said to me that he could have been the inspiration for the "serial foot stomper" subplot of *Polyester* and the entire premise of *Serial Mom,* but I have never discussed this with John Waters.

Later that year Glenn had to appear in court for writing a bad check. He had bought an antique crib for a friend who was expecting, and the check bounced. Glenn had kept this a secret from us, and we only found out when his attorney called to ask if Harris and I would come to the hearing.

Glenn was shocked to see his Dad and me in court. I never did tell him how we found out. Apparently, Glenn thought that as long as he had checks in the book, he could use them. The judge heard his story and gave him a year on probation. He was told to report to his probation officer once a month

Director and dear friend John Waters, photographed in Provincetown, August 1973

and to not leave the state.

The following New Year's Eve, I received a call from Glenn. He was in Times Square waiting for the big ball to drop. I reminded him of what the judge had said. "Don't worry, Mom," he said. "The probation officer lived two houses from us in Loch Raven Village. I went to school with him."

One day around this same time, I told our housekeeper, Mabel, that I would help her turn the mattress as she did spring cleaning. When we lifted the mattress on Glenn's bed, I saw what looked like a script for a play. I saw "Divine" and "David Lochary" written all over the top page. I put the papers back and forgot about them.

One day not long afterward, my friend Dolly had to go downtown. On the window of a store, I noticed a poster that also mentioned David Lochary and Divine. But I didn't know who Divine was. I meant to ask Glenn if David Lochary was taking up acting, but I forgot about it and never asked.

Glenn's friend Carol Wernig, of course, had introduced him to John Waters, who was running with a group of young beatniks downtown and had begun to make underground films. "Carol and I became friends," remembers John, "and she knew Divine, who was then Glenn and lived across the street with his parents, who had a nursery school. Having Divine as your only son is an odd advertisement for a nursery school, I guess. That's how I met him, through her. David Lochary and I met through Carol too. She

knew this whole pack, and they kind of hung downtown, and I took my pack of friends, which certainly included Mary Vivian Pearce and a lot of people we grew up with, and we started going downtown to Mardick's, which was kind of a beatnik bar. It was the only place in town where you could hang out with your friends, get served, and buy grass. And I met Pat Moran there. All the people that had come from their suburban neighborhoods to run away from conformist kids their own age met there.

"So it was a mixture of all classes, all sexualities. But they had one thing in common—they were angry, they had a good sense of humor, and they took drugs. That was another thing. During that time, 1964 to 1966, pot had just come out, and we did it kind of early...and it united us in a sense of humor, as marijuana always does, especially then when it was really not discussed and was very, very much underground.

"It became a family of sorts, and we made these 8-millimeter movies. Certainly, *Roman Candles* was basically home movies of our twisted extended family of choice. It was heavily influenced by Andy Warhol's *Chelsea Girls*, which was two 16-millimeter movies projected side by side at the same time. *Roman Candles* was three movies filmed in 8-millimeter and shown side by side at the same time and was stuff like Mink Stole playing at a grave, Divine playing hide-and-seek, and it starred Maelcum Soul, who was my first outlandish female star. It also had

"Then John started giving lectures where he'd introduce me as 'the

Pat Moran singing 'These Boots Were Made for Walking' and whipping her boyfriend of the time."

Chan Wilroy remembers Maelcum, who died in 1968, just as Divine's star was on the rise. "Maelcum was definitely the big cheese for a while. Unlike Glenn, she was as outrageous in real life as she was in Waters's movies. She would wear whiteface makeup, dress all in black, and generally affect the 'goth' look that wouldn't really catch on for another 30 years or so. At the time, we all thought she looked like she belonged on *The Munsters*. People have said that if Maelcum hadn't died, there never would have been a Divine, but I think that John and Glenn very early on had a unique artistic relationship that went way beyond the novelty that Glenn was in drag. He was totally unique as a performer and was the very first of his kind to be leading lady and make it work. Even John's detractors are forced to admit that Divine shines in those early films."

Glenn later told an interviewer about his first collaboration with John: "I was having a surprise birthday party for a friend of mine, and John was at the party. He had just gotten his first camera from his grandmother and had decided to try it out at this party. That's how I came to be in *Roman Candles*."

Just weeks before his death, Glenn recalled those early days of filmmaking in *Interview* magazine. "He [Waters] used his friends. He called me 'Divine' because he thought I was, and someone else was 'Mink

Stole.' Her real name was Nancy Stole; she lived around the corner. Someone else was 'Extreme Unction.' John was obsessed with film, so we would get together on Sunday afternoons and make movies. And then during the week we'd meet for Cokes and chips and watch them, and we thought we were the greatest things since sliced bread. It wasn't until they were shown at the University of Maryland and Georgetown University in film-making classes that we realized other people thought they were neat too.

"Then John started giving lectures where he'd introduce me as 'the most beautiful woman in the world, almost.' I would come out and have a 'modeling fit,' throw a fish at the audience—Baltimore is a big seafood town—and rip telephone books in half."

In a 1998 interview in the documentary film *Divine Trash,* John remembers how Glenn became Divine: "Divine must have been named after the character in Jean Genet's novel, *Our Lady of the Flowers,* but for years I didn't think it was. It was a Catholic word that the nuns in school used to repeat over and over: 'This is divine, and this is divine,' on and on. I didn't remember the thing in *Our Lady of the Flowers,* although that must be impossible because I was reading that book when I christened Glenn 'Divine'."

Of course, I had no idea that John and Glenn and the other kids were becoming stars among the Baltimore hippie crowd or that these movies, which I didn't even know

most beautiful woman in the world, almost.""

about, were being shown in, of all places, local churches!

John remembers, "We showed *Roman Candles* at an Episcopal Church, and Father Fred Hanna and another guy, Bill Bray, were the people who allowed me to rent that church hall, and they were very, very supportive, and they had gotten a lot of flack, I'm sure. In the '60s, it's easy to forget, religious people could be very left-wing, And they would let, for instance, Black Panthers meet in churches. So I guess they thought, *Well, anything to get these people in a church.* What other way would my audience ever come inside a church? So maybe that's why they let us do it.

"*Roman Candles* had a premiere at the annual Mt. Vernon Flower Mart, which was at the time a real straight thing for older ladies and flowers, but every freak in town went every year dressed in outrageous costumes to see who could scare people the most."

Father Fred Hanna, now a retired Episcopal priest, remembers the audience at the Roman Candles premiere: "When John showed the movie at Emmanuel, he tied it in with Kenneth Anger's *Eaux d'Artifice* (1953), which is a short film about a bunch of transvestites floating through a bunch of fountains in an elaborate garden, and I thought it was appropriate for Mt. Vernon Square. It was a lovely day, and we had a wonderful turnout. The audience members, here and at the subsequent movie premieres,

were better than the films, although don't tell John that. The audiences were wonderful. They were mixtures of Mount Vernon Club elderly dames, young faggots and hustlers, and of course a whole bunch of hippies. This was the '60s, and Mt. Vernon Square was filled with hippies every day."

Harvey Alexander, who was teaching film history at the University of Baltimore at the time, remembers the student film scene in the late '60s. "Experimental films were being shown in Baltimore, and they were being made at the Maryland Institute, Towson State, and the University of Maryland in Baltimore County. Also, there were some people hanging out at Fells Point (a downscale waterfront neighborhood where years later the television series *Homicide* would be filmed) who were making films. But all of these groups were kind of disorganized. No one was getting together to put the films in one place where a lot of people could see them, and so these experimental films were being seen usually by the friends of the people who made them."

Another local film professor, Dr. Richard Macksey of Johns Hopkins University, agrees. "The film scene was emerging, and there was some genuine talent floating around. But as far as anything that you could call a community, it really didn't exist yet. Around the time of John's first movies with Divine, *Roman Candles* and *Eat Your Makeup*, we had just started a cooperative film festival—Goucher College, the Maryland Institute

College of Art, and Hopkins—and one of the films submitted was in fact *Eat Your Makeup,* and this was my first contact with John. This was the sort of film festival where friends of the filmmakers and the filmmakers would start fistfights, depending on how the prize awards went.

"People didn't know what to make of *Eat Your Makeup,* much less what to make of Divine, who was playing Jackie Kennedy in a parody of the Kennedy assassination. In fact, he was the first actor to play Jackie in a film.

"My students, who were terribly interested in the technology of films, were shocked by John's film. They weren't shocked by the content; they were shocked by the fact that John seemed, in a sense, never to have discovered the light meter. So at that point, John had a profoundly ironic relationship to his own work. John didn't win any awards in that festival, I might add."

In the summer of 1966, around the time of *Roman Candles* and *Eat Your Makeup,* Harris and I decided to go to Puerto Rico. We made Glenn promise to not have a party while we were gone. When we arrived in Puerto Rico, he called to see if we'd arrived. After he hung up, I thought, *Oh, no.* After a week's stay in San Juan, we arrived home. Everyone was happy. Glenn said he'd gone to work every day and that everything had gone well. Then I received another florist bill, this time for over $800. I threw the bill at Glenn and told him I was not going to pay it. He just looked at me, smiled, and batted his eyes.

While Glenn lived at home, there was never a dull moment. He told us one day he had decided to go to the University of Maryland to study interior design. I gave him the $150 entrance fee and money for his supplies. But I noticed that he never brought any work or papers home. Not surprisingly, I started to get suspicious. One day he was having work done on his car and had borrowed mine. That evening I called Dolly and asked if she would take me down to the university to see where Glenn had parked my car. My excuse was that I needed something out of the glove compartment. She drove me there, and we drove around the school, but we couldn't find the car.

The next morning, I asked Glenn if he parked my car in a safe place. "Oh, yeah, Mom," he said. "I parked it in the church parking lot across the street." I wanted to believe him, but I didn't. So the following school night, Dolly and I played cops and robbers again. My car was nowhere around the church or school. We decided to sit in the car and wait for the students to come out of class. And guess what? No Glenn. When Harris and I confronted him, he just laughed. I told him he couldn't have my car to run around in anymore.

Harris and I were getting increasingly

Glenn as Jackie Kennedy covering JFK in Eat Your Makeup

frustrated at this point. Glenn was a talented and smart young man, but he seemed to have no concept of adult responsibility. We thought that maybe if he had a hair styling business of his own, with us involved, he might be able to learn about money management. I had begun doing a little hairdressing myself, and with me overseeing and participating, maybe Glenn would grow up a little. So we decided to surprise him by buying him a beauty shop in Ruxton Towers on Charles Street in Towson.

When we told him, he said he was tired of doing hair, that it made him nervous, and that he just did it to please me, which wasn't true. I asked Salvatore to go into partnership with me since Glenn wasn't interested. I liked Salvatore, and I knew I could trust him. Glenn couldn't have cared less. He did come to work there, though, and he had his own styling room.

One day I was in the neighborhood grocery store, and as I rounded the corner of one of the aisles, I saw from behind a huge henna bouffant, which I instantly recognized as belonging to one of Glenn's regular clients. She was having a conversation with another woman, and I walked toward her to say hello. As I got closer, I heard her say, "Yeah, I know he does a great job on my hair. I wouldn't go to anyone else. But you know, he doesn't like girls. I mean, he's obviously a queer."

"You bitch," I hissed. "My son is a human being with feelings just like yours."

She turned around, and her eyes opened wide.

"If my son is so troubling to you, you should find someplace else to get your hair done." I stormed past and got out of the store as fast as I could.

I never told Glenn about the remark because I knew it would hurt his feelings. Still, I'm sure that I was unable to protect him from all of the comments aimed at him. And I know that *Multiple Maniacs* has a beehived suburban woman who says, "I've known a coupla queers. In fact, I think my hairdresser's queer," and *Female Trouble* is loaded with jokes about Gator, the nongay hairdresser. So I guess Glenn, John, and David Lochary were aware of this bigotry.

Most of Glenn's customers, though, were very fond of him. He had one customer who was pregnant and said to him, "I hope my baby is born with eyes like yours." She was one of Glenn's favorite customers.

Another lady attending the Johnson inaugural ball wanted a hairdo like Marie Antoinette. She was young, and she looked magnificent, but we later heard that once she got to the event, she was unable to get through the door of the dining room because Glenn had built up her wig so high.

When we would make comments on his customers' hair, Glenn would always say, "I'm the star, so eat your hearts out."

One day I received a liquor store bill in the mail. Harris and I didn't drink, so I called the store and asked for the manager, who

I went up to his bedroom and looked under his mattress, and there Belvedere, complete with an arch and a champagne fountain.

was one of Glenn's customers. She told me that Glenn had given her a bad check. I was flabbergasted. Glenn was already on probation for writing one bad check. She also told me that the liquor was for a party he'd had at the Sheraton Hotel. Instead of dealing with the situation, Glenn had gotten angry at her for "having a big mouth" and told her not to come into the beauty shop anymore.

Around this same time, I received a third bill from the Towson Florist. I called and told them that I had warned them before to get their money up front, and I refused to pay. I later said to Harris, "I wonder what the hell is going to happen next."

In the summer of 1968, Glenn decided to rent an apartment. Although we did not know it at the time, he had already appeared in some of John Waters's early movies. When Glenn told us his plans, his dad and I were really happy. We thought that maybe this would instill some responsibility in him. We gave him the money to pay the rent for the first couple of months, and off he went. He occupied this first apartment, in Ellicott City, so briefly that Harris and I never even saw it. John Waters later told me that the landlady got angry with Glenn when she noticed he'd torn down the drapes and done something different without her permission. He thought he was doing a good deed. I later learned that all of Glenn's movie friends were living in hippie communes in the woods at this time. I sometimes wonder if he ever lived out there too. I really can't picture

him doing that.

After being kicked out of his first apartment, Glenn moved to Park Avenue in Baltimore. After he had finished decorating his new home, he invited Grandma Milstead, Harris, and me to dinner. His new apartment had three balconies, each with a lighted Christmas tree. Traffic on Park Avenue slowed down just to admire the trees, which could be seen from the street. The entire apartment was decorated beautifully, and the dinner was delicious.

For New Year's Eve, 1968-69, Glenn had planned a big party at the Belvedere Hotel, for which he had reserved a banquet room many months in advance, when he was still living at home with Harris and me. A woman from the Belvedere called and told me that Glenn really knew how to have a party. This was the first I'd heard of it. I said, "Lady, if you want your money, you'd better get it up front, because I'm not going to pay any more of his bills." She told me he had ordered flowers, a band, food, and champagne fountains. She said Perle Mesta, the Washington, D.C., socialite, had nothing on Glenn.

I went up to his bedroom and looked under his mattress, and there it was: a reservation for a party of 500 on New Year's Eve at the Belvedere, complete with an arch and a champagne fountain. The bill for the deposit, not counting flowers, was $2500. The flowers were another $800.

That night, Glenn came over for dinner.

it was: a reservation for a party of 500 on New Year's Eve at the

"What was your day like, Mom?" he asked, batting his blue eyes.

"As a matter of fact, Glenny, I saw a psychic today. She told me that the next time I receive a bill in the mail, you will be going on a long trip to jail."

He called the Belvedere lady the next day and cut the party down to a mere 200 guests. He must have paid the bill, because she never sent it to me.

I did, however, shortly after New Years, receive a bill from the Williamson Electric Company for $1500 for a chandelier Glenn had had installed in his apartment on Park Avenue. I told him he had to send it back if he couldn't afford to buy it, so he returned it.

"I used to see Glenn at parties," remembers film historian Harvey Alexander, who had met Glenn through John and the other film people. "I felt comfortable with him. I mean, I liked him better really when he was not in drag. He just seemed to be someone who wanted to make people laugh. Some of the funniest things I've ever heard anyone say were said by Glenn at parties. He did his little 'I'm a Little Teapot' imitation. I mean, he really was an entertainer. He could have walked on a stage anywhere and gotten people to like him and to laugh not at him, but with him. And he was quite a social person. I can't say that I spent a lot of time in his presence, but the time that I did see him,

I never saw a mopey person. I mean, he just seemed to enjoy life for all that it had to offer."

This was around the time that Harris's increasing stiffness and lack of mobility was finally diagnosed as muscular dystrophy. He began to walk with a cane, and I was terrified that he might have an accident. Because of that and all of the worry about Glenn, I developed an ulcer. The doctor sent me to Union Memorial Hospital for tests. Glenn came in to see me and brought me a dozen red roses and a bottle of Joy perfume. It made me happy until I went home and got the bill.

If Glenn had been arrested during this period—and he almost was—it might have been too much for Harris and me to handle, especially so soon after the Sally Crough murder ordeal. Mink Stole, who was in most of John's earlier movies and has been a wonderful friend to me since Glenn's death, remembers this story. "While we were filming *Mondo Trasho*," she says, "there was a scene where Divine picked up an imagined nude hitchhiker. She imagined the hitchhiker was nude. Well, in order for that to appear on film, you actually had to have a nude hitchhiker. So we had gone to the campus of Johns Hopkins University in Charles Village, thinking that would be a perfect spot to film. We got Mark Isherwood, the actor, to the location. He had a robe on most of the time, but there was the moment on film where he had to drop his robe and be naked."

John Waters, who describes *Mondo Trasho*

as "one horrible day in Divine's life when she accidentally ran over Bonnie Pearce," picks up the story. "So Mark took his clothes off, we got the shot, and a security guard called the police. The cops came, and we ran. Divine escaped, dressed in a gold-lamé toreador outfit, driving a red 1959 Cadillac El Dorado with the top down and a nude man in the front seat. And the police couldn't find them, which does not say a lot for the Baltimore City Police Department. We all escaped, but the next day they arrested Mark Isherwood, and then they came to our house and arrested everyone there for conspiracy to commit indecent exposure. Divine was never identified. Mink was also arrested."

"It was kind of interesting," Mink remembers. "When the police came to my door, I actually didn't know what they were there for. I had also been involved with somebody the day before who had been shoplifting, so I wasn't sure why they came. I heard this knock on the door—I was in the bathtub, and I heard the knock on the door, and my roommate answered the door, and it was the police, and I knew they were there for me, so I stayed very, very quiet in the tub. I didn't want anybody to know I was there. And they came in and they asked for me and nobody said anything, and then suddenly the bathroom door flew open, and there were these two policemen standing there. And I was like, 'Excuse me, I'm taking a bath!' They allowed me to get dressed, and then they hauled me down to the jail, where I found out that it wasn't shoplifting I was there for; it was the indecent exposure thing in the movie. John and David were already in cells."

"Except for Glenn, we all got busted," says John. "David Lochary made me a paper fan out of a gum wrapper and passed it down to me from his cell. It was very Genet. I had one phone call, and for reasons I can't imagine I called the ACLU, and it happened to be Judge Elizabeth Bothe, head of the ACLU, who answered the phone. It turned out to be the day that they decided which case they were going to pick. Total luck. And they picked our case to handle. So Fred Weisgal, who was a pretty famous Baltimore attorney, took the case, and it turned into a trial that got huge publicity. It was on the cover of *Variety*. The headline was 'Balto Mondo Trasho in Campus Pincho of Fig-Leafed Hero.' Me and my codefendants got off, and Judge Solomon Liss read us a poem, which was printed in the paper:

> *Old Baltimore's in a spin*
> *Because of Isherwood's display of skin.*
> *He cannot bear the shame and cracks*
> *Brought on by showing the bare facts.*
> *And so, go then and sin no more.*
> *Disrobe, if need be, behind the door.*
> *And if again, you heed the call to art,*
> *Rest assured, the judge will do his part.*

"It was kind of embarrassing because they printed my real name in the paper," Mink recalls, "along with my mother's address, which was not where I was living. I was living someplace else. But they printed my mother's address. My mother started getting phone calls from porno people looking for me to appear in their movies. And she was really upset. And then they started asking for my sister and then my younger sister. So that was a pretty serious issue for my mom for a while. "It said 'Nancy Stole, drugstore clerk,' with my mother's address.

"But I had a good quote. When we were actually at the police station and there were reporters around, one of the reporters asked me what happened, and I said there was more exposure in the arrest than in the incident, and they printed that in the paper."

Fortunately, Glenn somehow managed to not get arrested for this, even though practically everyone else did. I'm glad I didn't hear about this incident until years after the fact.

One day Glenn came home and told his dad and me that he hated doing hair and wanted to go into the thrift shop business and move to Provincetown on Cape Cod. So we all went shopping in antique stores, flea markets, and garage sales. We bought secondhand fur coats from the furriers. Harris decided to buy a new Volkswagen bus for the nursery, and we gave Glenn the old one

54

to use to haul his things. He didn't have it long before he overturned it. After that we bought him a new Chevrolet station wagon. It was beautiful—aqua and white—and he loved it.

About a year later Glenn invited Grandma, Dad, and me to Provincetown for the Thanksgiving holiday. We had a great time shopping for groceries and used things for his store. Glenn had his little store in the house where we stayed. It was cute. The things were all displayed beautifully. I prepared the turkey dinner, and the next day I went to the grocery store to load up his freezer. I didn't want him to be without food. Then he took us on a tour around the cape, and we bought dozens of candles, cranberry sauces, and Christmas decorations for me to take home. We left after three days. Just before we left, I asked the question I had been holding in all weekend: "Glenn, why in the hell did you cut your hair like that—short on the sides and shaved to the crown?"

He didn't answer.

John Waters gave the answer years later to interviewer Steve Yeager in the documentary film, *Divine Trash*. "It was to give more room for eye makeup. The human head did not have enough room for the eyebrows that we had in mind."

"The name of Glenn's shop in Provincetown shop was Divine Trash. That's where Steve got the idea for the title of his movie—not many people know that," Channing Wilroy told me. (Prior to that, in Baltimore,

Pat Moran's thrift shop was also named Divine Trash.) "I remember that the sign was carved into a quarter board, those inlaid carved wooden signs modeled on the woodwork signage of 19th-century ships. He had the shop in two places in two years there in P-town. The first place he had it, in 1970, was in an old house down at the end of Bradford Street where Pucci's Restaurant was. It had been a restaurant called the Penny Farthing. And Cookie Mueller (who was in several of John's early movies), Divine, his friend Spider, and I lived there. He had the shop in half of the downstairs in what had been the big living room/dining room area.

"He was there working in the shop every day during the day. We didn't get much business because he had opened it in the fall after the tourist season. The shop didn't stay open that long, because pretty soon the town came by and said, 'Where's your license?' Of course Div didn't have one. It was open, I think, for just one winter, and that was the end of that. But you can't really blame the city or the license issue, because he never had the rent, and it was only a matter of time before he would have been kicked out anyway.

"From there, he went to work for Patti Cozzi in a health food store. Glenn in a health food store—now there's some irony. The shop sold very expensive health food and upper-end cooking utensils. You could get ginseng, vitamins—that sort of thing. It was a one-person store, so while Glenn was there, he would do the stock, run the register, and wait on customers. This lasted a little under a year, until the beginning of the next tourist season. Then he opened up his second Divine Trash store, this time next to the old Muse restaurant. Again, he wasn't making enough profit to pay the rent. So around the end of the tourist season, when it was obvious that he wasn't going to get anywhere with the shop, he sold all of the stock at bottom-of-the-barrel prices and closed up.

"But his salesmanship wasn't over yet. He still didn't have enough money to pay the rent on his furnished apartment, and it was time for him to move out. So when the landlady went out of town for the weekend, Glenn had an auction and sold off all her furniture. Nobody knew what he was doing— not the buyers, not the auctioneer, certainly not the landlady. So she came back to town and looked for her furniture and found out what had happened. She put out a warrant, and that's when he left town. He had to blow town for seven years. He didn't come back until 1978-79, when he was starring in *Neon Woman* at the Pilgrim House Theatre.

"Over those couple of years, I lived with Glenn in three different places in Provincetown. He slept late— very, very late—but he was easy to get along with. I loved living with Glenny. He loved to cook, so there

was always great food to eat, and he loved to clean. It was fabulous. And of course he was a lot of fun. He always had some really great grass too.

"But Glenny was not the most up-and-up person in the world. When Spider and Glenn were living together at the Esplanade, the guy who lived below them had a party and invited them to come. They went to the party and saw that this guy had a beautiful and fabulously expensive oriental rug. Glenn wanted the

56

"I looked up and saw a 250-pound man with a shaved head in ful
protect him from the snow and wind. I'm pretty sure it must have

rug, and he talked about it all the time. When the guy went off on vacation, Glenn and Spider went out over the balcony on the outside of the building and went into his apartment through his balcony down below. What passersby must have thought as they saw Glenn, all 250 pounds of him, crawling down the side of the building, I can't imagine. They moved the furniture in the guy's place, rolled up the rug, took it out, and took it up over the balcony. Then they put it down in their own apartment.

"When the guy got back, he reported the rug missing, and the police came in and made out a report on this rare and expensive oriental rug. The cops even asked around the building if anyone had seen anything, but I don't know if they ever talked to Glenn or Spider. Later, something happened in Glenn's apartment with the plumbing. He called the maintenance people, and the maintenance guy came up to fix the plumbing and recognized the rug. Glenn recognized on the spot that the guy was looking at the rug and probably knew whose it was. Glenn knew he was going to be toast. So the guy fixed the plumbing and left the apartment. When he left, Glenn and Spider immediately rolled the rug up and took it back outside through the window, down over the balcony, and back into the guy's apartment."

One of Glenn's closest friends, Anne Cersosimo, recalls seeing Divine around this time. "Divine and I did not become friends until the mid '80s when he toured Europe

with his nightclub act," she says, "but I am almost certain I saw him in Provincetown during the winter one year. I remember getting into a fight with my husband and storming out of the house in the middle of a blizzard. While walking off my anger, I looked up and saw a 250-pound man with a shaved head in full drag walking down the street with only a bright red parasol to protect him from the snow and wind. I'm pretty sure it must have been Divine."

Little did Harris and I know that even while Glenn was planning his move to Provincetown, John and he were shooting another movie in Baltimore. *The Diane Linkletter Story* was a short movie shot in one day in 1969 to test a sound camera that John wanted to use on his next feature.

"It dramatized an actual event," recalls Harvey Alexander, who screened the movie at his first Baltimore Film Festival. "Art Linkletter's daughter had committed suicide while under the influence of LSD, and the story was all over the newspapers. John turned the story into a black comedy, with Divine playing Diane Linkletter and David Lochary and Bonnie Pearce playing her parents. After an argument with them about her hippie boyfriend Jim—whom we never see—Diane runs up to her room and moons all over a photograph of Jim, kissing and crying all over it. Finally, she leaps out of the window to

rag walking down the street with only a bright red parasol to
een Divine."

her death. Divine really chews up the scenery in his first speaking role. He's covered in love beads, which clatter as he moves around, and you can clearly see a day or two of stubble on his face. He comes off like a cross-dressing hippie version of Liz Taylor in *Butterfield 8*."

Glenn's next film is one I've never seen. He talked about it in an interview, though, shortly after its premiere. "I think my greatest performance to date has been in *Multiple Maniacs*. It was our first sound feature. In that one, I have the Cavalcade of Perversions, where we travel all around terrifying people, making them sick with the various acts we have. Then, at the end, I'm lying around not knowing what to do. And then I'm attacked and raped by this lobster, Lobstora. And then I crawl out onto the street in Fell's Point and terrorize people before I'm shot to death by the National Guard."

The most controversial and famous scene in *Multiple Maniacs* is when "Lady Divine" has an intimate moment, "the rosary bead moment," with a scarfed and rosary-swinging Mink Stole in the pews of an actual church.

George Figgs is a movie theater owner, film historian, and longtime friend of John Waters. He is one of the original Dreamlanders, John's troop of actor/cohorts. George describes the scene: "I was Jesus Christ during the 'bead job' scene. There's a 'fever dream,' an ecstatic dream that is being had while the beads are supposedly being pulled out of Divine's butthole. The scene was simu-

lated, of course, but still it went to new heights of blasphemy. The bead job scene cannot be topped. It really got people's attention. I just think that's the most outrageous and blasphemous thing that anyone, including myself, has ever seen or ever will see."

Amazingly, most of the early screenings of this film took place in churches. Lou Cedrone, who covered many of these church screenings for the *Baltimore Sun*, recalls his first reaction to *Multiple Maniacs*: "When Divine took the rosary and did obscene things with it, I thought, *Well, there you go*. By this point I was no longer shocked by anything that John and his Dreamlanders did."

John Waters has pointed out that the Maryland State Film Censor Board was only able to see *Multiple Maniacs* years later, and they had no authority over movies shown at churches. "We didn't have any censorship problems with that movie because we showed it in churches. At that point, we were doing this on purpose. Still, I remember standing with David Lochary in front of the church waiting for the bust that we thought was going to happen—but didn't because the police were not going to raid a church.

"The Maryland Censor Board could only hassle us if we played in commercial theaters. So even when *Pink Flamingos* finally opened and I had the first world premiere on the University of Baltimore campus, it was out of the board's jurisdiction.

"Ten years later in 1981, *Multiple Maniacs* played at the Charles Theater, an

Divine is led to spiritual enlightenment by The Infant of Prague in John Waters' Multiple Maniacs, 1970

art house downtown, and the Censor Board finally had to see it. There was a huge article in the paper that really caused me trouble at the time because it was right when we were making *Polyester,* and we were trying to talk the neighbors into letting us shoot in this upscale neighborhood. We're telling them, 'Oh, don't worry. It's just a comedy about suburbia.' Meanwhile there's this huge article in the paper about the judge sitting through it and saying things like, 'My eyes were insulted for 90 minutes, but it doesn't seem to be illegal.' Mary Avara, chair of the Censor Board and the last film censor in America, was flipping out, saying it was the most obscene thing she'd ever seen. Even though it came at the worst imaginable time, it made me laugh that she had to sit there and watch it."

Mary Avara wasn't laughing though, even 15 years later. "Oh, my gosh. That was disgraceful—sacrilegious and everything," she said to an interviewer in 1996. "I was sick over that…They had sex in a church? My God… It was unreal. Filthy. I had my own rating: RT—real trash."

Lou Cedrone looked back on the long fight between John and Mary Avara, which didn't end until the Censor Board was abolished in the '80s and said, "Mary did have some say in what films were passed, and she insisted that they cut a couple of scenes from *Multiple Maniacs, Pink Flamingos, and Female Trouble.* But when it comes to being a censor with a John Waters film, the fact that you let it get through in any form imaginable is a sign that you've been defeated, really. Mary did say, 'If I could have made Waters cut that dog-doo eating scene at the end of *Pink Flamingos,* he'd 'a had a whole different career.' And I think she's right!"

People might ask how Harris and I could remain unaware of this stuff, which was splashed all over the papers in Baltimore. But the truth is, with Harris slowing down and having trouble walking and the day-to-day worries about what Glenn was up to, we weren't looking at the newspaper much at all, certainly not at the police reports or the movie section.

Glenn did call us quite often so we wouldn't worry about him. But we felt sometimes he didn't know what he wanted to do, just like a mixed-up kid. I even thought it was me and talked to a psychiatrist about Glenn and myself. The doctor told me that maybe Glenn was hiding something from us and wanted to get away from us because he was afraid we might find out. Of course the doctor was right, but I couldn't believe that at the time.

CHAPTER 4

"I will be queen one day, and the coronation will be celebrated all over the world. Do not forget, I AM DIVINE!"

—Babs Johnson (Divine) in *Pink Flamingos* (1972)

While Glenn's career was taking off, Harris and I had no idea what was going on in his life. It wasn't until after our reconciliation and after Glenn's death that we became fully aware of his years of hard work on movies and the stage.

Of course, the movie that made John and Glenn famous is *Pink Flamingos,* a film about the battle for the title of "the filthiest people alive." The family of Babs Johnson (Divine) battles the evil couple Connie and Raymond Marble, played by Mink Stole and David Lochary. The movie has become a cult classic all over the world because of its outrageousness.

I have never seen the film, and I don't think I ever will. Glenn asked me not to, and it doesn't sound like the sort of movie I would like. A couple of years before he died, I asked Glenn if it was true what people said about the film. He just looked at me with that twinkle in his blue eyes, laughed, and said, "Mom, you wouldn't believe what they can do nowadays with trick photography." I will continue to respect Glenn's wish that I not watch that movie, because as long as I do, it can remain just trick photography.

In the months before our painful separation from Glenn, he and the rest of the movie kids were working around the clock to get *Pink Flamingos* finished. Over the years, I have heard many stories of how hard it was to get that movie made, and how hard Glenn worked with John and the other actors. I still can't imagine my Glenn, who had expensive taste in clothes and furniture and food, abiding the pitiful conditions that I have heard everyone endured while making the movie. Sometimes I wonder if the stress involved in making that movie and the decisions Glenn had to make about what John was asking him to do added to the stress and secrecy of his relationship with Harris and me.

"When he wasn't up in Provincetown with John and the other Dreamland people," remembers Glenn's good friend Bob Adams, "Divine was living in this beautiful apartment on Park Avenue in Baltimore with floor-to-ceiling drapes and a huge chandelier that hung from the ceiling until his mother made him take it back to the store. Suddenly, for the filming of *Pink Flamingos,* he was forced to come out to our hippie commune in Phoenix, Maryland, where John and Vince Peranio

On the set of Pink Flamingos

had built the trailer set. Divine had to walk a mile out to the set in his heels. We didn't have any hot water in the farmhouse, so any washing up or shaving he and Van Smith had to do to get him ready took place with cold water. After a while, they started crashing at Susan Lowe's place in the city, and they'd get up before dawn with Van making Divy up and dressing him in full costume for Jack Walsh to drive him out to the set. Sometimes Divy would have to wait out front in full drag for Jack to pull the car around from back, and cars full of these blue-collar types on their way to work would practically mount the pavement from gawking at him."

John Waters still has fond memories of the close-knit group of people who worked on Pink Flamingos, and he remembers well his careful crafting of Glenn's performance as Babs Johnson. "When the people joined up to make *Pink Flamingos,* they didn't do it like actors to make a movie. It was like volunteering to help commit a crime. It was like driving the getaway car or blowing out the security camera. It was like joyously committing a culture crime. And I think that was the spirit that everybody joined in to make that movie. Even Divine—now, Divine was no hippie at all, believe me. But he had that anger underneath, and I was able to tap into that and write lines that brought it out.

"There really was no improvisation in the movie at all. These people weren't playing any version of themselves—certainly not Divine—and they weren't improvising on a

character. This was a written script, and we had rehearsals for about a month before we shot it. We rehearsed it like a play in my apartment. I would go around and pick everybody up at night for rehearsal and bring them over. When we started to shoot, the scripts were handwritten. They weren't even typed. It was long, long dialogue that they had in that movie, more than any movie I would ever make now. People never shut up. They just rant, rant, rant, and it gives you a headache just to listen to them.

"*Multiple Maniacs* and *Pink Flamingos* were both shot with TV newsreel cameras with the magnetic stripe on the edge of the film. You just ran the film through the camera and the sound was recorded right on the film as it ran. So there were no cuts. We had to shoot one whole scene, three or four pages at one time without making one mistake.

"I got a lot of help from newscasters with equipment from TV stations—I never asked if the TV stations knew about it. It was usually on the cameraman's day off. Brad Ganson from Channel 13 in Baltimore provided the camera for most of the shooting of *Pink Flamingos.*"

Brad Ganson still laughs when he thinks about shooting *Pink Flamingos.* "I would bring all of the gear to the set—the camera, the lights, the microphones, the sound box, and everything—and set it all up for John. He did the actual filming. As for what I saw during the shooting of *Pink Flamingos,* most of it was new to me."

John Waters filming Pink Flamingos, *1972*

Mary Vivian Pearce, who played Divine's peroxide-blond "traveling companion" Cotton in *Pink Flamingos*, recalls how hard it was to get the movie made: "Those scenes that were shot out by the trailer in the woods were incredibly grueling. We could only shoot on weekends because those were the TV station cameraman's days off from work. This was in the middle of January. The whole thing was shot outdoors. It was rehearse, rehearse, rehearse until we got it right, and then John and the cameraman, Brad Ganson, would shoot the whole scene—pages and pages of dialogue—in one take. Divine would be there in his skimpy, skintight

dress with his goose bumps showing because it was so cold. He was always totally focused and professional, though.

"There was no food to be found anywhere, and you know how that must have affected him. We never took any food up there. We'd just not eat and shoot all day, smoke cigarettes, and take speed. Edith always had some really good speed. We'd just split that up, so there was no need for food, just cigarettes.

"I was there for the shooting of the final scene. It was the very last thing we shot, and John has told the story of how the dog had stage fright and Glenn had to wait on the

In between takes on the set of Pink Flamingos, *1972*

street in full costume and makeup while John and Danny Mills followed the dog around with the camera. The poor dog was really having star fits. We ended up having to use a hair-dye applicator bottle to give this little poodle an enema to try and make it shit, and it still didn't. We were following it around with a camera and Divine was sweating through his heavy costume and makeup, even though it was really cold—freezing—out that day. At one point, this straight-looking couple in their 30s came around the corner walking their dog, and John yelled after them, 'Hey, does that dog need to shit?' Finally, the dog squatted, and Divine said, 'Is that it?' and we said, 'Yes, that's it!' and Divine gave this great shit-eating grin. When it was all over and the scene was in the can, I looked at Divine and thought, 'Now that is one game actor.'

"Later that night, we were all at Paul Swift's apartment, the guy who plays the Egg Man in the movie, and we were smoking some very strong marijuana, and someone said you could get real sick from eating dog shit. Divine got more and more uptight. Finally, he went into the next room and picked up the phone and called Johns Hopkins Hospital. We all listened in to his side of the conversation: 'White worm? What's white worm?... Oh, my God!... No, it's my son, he's 12 years old.... Yes, well, he's a little retarded.' We all erupted into laughter."

In 1974, Glenn spoke to a Baltimore reporter about the scene: "Why did I do it?

Because it was in the script. That is the only reason I did it. John had asked me a year or so before if I would, and I said I would. And the day came to do it. It was such a strange day because I followed that dog around for three hours just zooming in on its asshole. Now people always comment about that scene. Like I said, people think I just run around doing it all the time. I've received boxes of dog shit—plastic dog shit. I have gone to parties where people just sit around and talk about dog shit because they think it's what I want to talk about. People think I'm into a whole scene, and a lot of people think John is too. But people always ask about it or comment on it. They liked it in the movie, I guess."

John has said, "The whole humor of the movie is about pot. I wrote it on pot, the audience was on pot, and when Divine said, yes, he'd eat dog shit, he was on pot. It's a first, and it's a last in cinema history. There's no law against it, because no one's ever going to do it again. It's not even in the Bible. It's not even a sin in Catholicism to eat shit. Because who would want to, and who will again?"

Pat Moran is John's oldest friend, casting director, and associate producer. Her son, Brook Yeaton, is Divine's godson. Brook remembers that his dog was Glenn's costar that day. "Later Glenn said it was the most disgusting thing he'd ever done in his life. And he also told me to be prepared to do that if I want a career in film in any aspect.

Every time that I would complain about the hours or trying to get my career started, he would say, 'Well, look what I did.'

"Divine was a serious actor, though, because when you watch any of his films, the first couple of scenes you'll say to yourself, *That's a man in a dress*. But by the fourth or fifth scene, you don't even see it. He always took you away from that stereotype, and you watched Divine—you watched a woman on screen."

Harvey Alexander says, "I think Glenn was a really decent human being, and I think he wanted to act and John was his director. It was a relationship that worked. I don't know what John would have done without Glenn. I can't even begin to speculate. But I think that Glenn and John, I think their success is kind of mutual. I think the one fed the other in some sense.

"I was the first person to show *Pink Flamingos* in Baltimore. This was late 1972, and I had never seen it, but there was a tremendous amount of energy surrounding it. You couldn't go anywhere in this city without meeting someone who knew someone working on it or who'd heard about it. At this point, I was still teaching English and film theory at University of Baltimore, and it was time for the Third Annual Baltimore Film Festival. We needed a lot of publicity, so I asked John if he would like to screen *Flamingos*. Until this time, his screenings had been in church basements and the like. So we had a room at the Langsdale Auditorium

here on the University of Baltimore campus where they actually had a projection booth and about 500 seats, and I asked the Dean of the school if it would be all right. His concern was very much like mine, that we had to generate some income for the film festival.

"So the night came, and the night after, and the night after that, and he sold out every performance. I was never surprised at the later success of John and Glenn's films because of the tremendous success of those screenings. I could understand one performance being sold out, or the first night being sold out, but every night was completely sold out. Traffic was absolutely unbearable, and the lines went down and around the block in the freezing cold. Where did they park? I have no idea, but people came! And sitting in the audience watching the film—my God, I had never seen anything like it.

"The end of the film, where Divine follows the dog around and then…gulp! I must admit I really lost it. I mean, I couldn't believe I was seeing that. And I did some serious dry heaving. And for some reason, because I could do the dry heaves I felt in a way liberated. I kept thinking, 'This is about as free as it gets!'

"Glenn was surprised by all of this," Harvey continues. "John and Glenn had begun making personal appearances in New York, San Francisco, Philadelphia, and other cities to promote *Multiple Maniacs* a year or so before, and Divine was beginning to be recognized as something of a cult celebrity."

Glenn later said, "I hadn't even seriously considered a career in showbiz or entertainment. We just made the first movies for fun, you know. It was almost just kidding around. And then each one grew a little more and got more of a following, and more people wanted to see it—until *Pink Flamingos*. Well, *Pink Flamingos* sat on the shelf for a year, and we all thought that nothing was ever going to come of it. It was very upsetting."

But fame for the Dreamlanders was not a long way off. George Figgs characterizes the road to fame thusly: "When people heard there was a drag queen eating dog shit in an underground film, it went out over the wire services. And it became 'The Gulp Heard 'Round the World.' That was the real breakthrough."

Around the same time that *Pink Flamingos* was being made, the doctor told me that if Harris wanted a long life, we should move to a warm climate. His health was a big worry for both of us, and only added to our worries about Glenn, whom we almost never heard from. Then one day we received a call from Salvatore, who was vacationing at his winter home in Florida. He told us he'd seen Glenn and a few friends in Florida antique hunting. He had invited

Steve Yeager (left, with beard) as a reporter in a tense scene from Pink Flamingos.

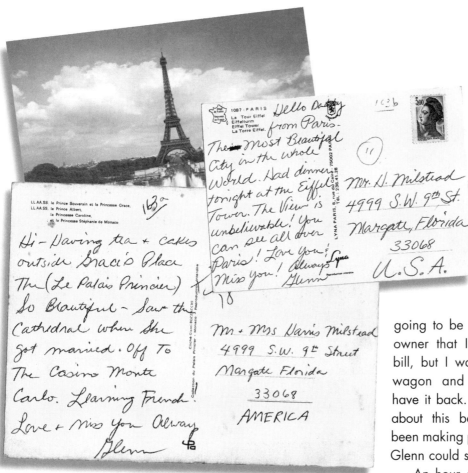

Postcard 1 (printed): LL.AA.SS. le Prince Souverain et la Princesse Grace. LL.AA.SS. le Prince Albert, la Princesse Caroline, et la Princesse Stéphanie de Monaco.

Hi – Having tea + cakes outside Grace's Place The (Le Palais Princier) So Beautiful – Saw the Cathedral where She got married. Off To The Casino Monte Carlo. Learning French! Love + Miss You Always Glenn

Mr + Mrs Harris Milstead
4999 S.W. 9th Street
Margate Florida
33068
AMERICA

Postcard 2 (printed): 1087 - PARIS / La Tour Eiffel / Eiffelturm / Eiffel Tower / La Torre Eiffel

Hello Daddy from Paris- The most Beautiful City in the whole World. Had dinner tonight at the Eiffel Tower. The View is unbelievable! You can see all over Paris! Love you! Miss you! Always Glenn

Mr. H. Milstead
4999 S.W. 9th St.
Margate, Florida
33068
U.S.A.

them to dinner, but they never showed up. Salvatore was angry and said he would never invite him again. I was getting to that point myself.

The final straw was when I had to go to the gas station a week later. I knew the owner, and while I was getting gas, he told me that Glenn had burned up the Chevy station wagon's transmission while driving home from Florida. He said that the wagon was there being fixed. I asked if Glenn was going to pay the bill, and the owner said Glenn had told him to make the bill out to Harris.

On my way home, I thought about Glenn stopping at the gas station, three blocks away from our house, and not bothering to stop in and see how we were doing. I became so angry with him that when I got home, I told Harris about it. Harris was upset too and said, "The more we do for Glenn, the less he appreciates us." He made me call the garage to find out when the car was going to be ready. I told the owner that I would pay the bill, but I wanted the station wagon and Glenn couldn't have it back. I didn't feel bad about this because we had been making payments on it so Glenn could save his money.

An hour after I picked up the car, Glenn called and asked if he could have it back. I said, "No, Glenn, you have used us long enough. You think more of your friends than your parents, so you can ask them to get you back to Provincetown. What are you really up to there anyway?"

He said, "I'm making a movie, and I'm Marie Antoinette."

"Well, then I hope they do a good job when they cut off your head," I snapped back. "Don't come back. Don't tell anyone you have a father or mother, and leave us alone."

I cried for a month after that. Then Glenn came to the house with a couple of his friends. He asked Harris for the car. Harris told him that he didn't appreciate Glenn's behavior and that Glenn could have come home and discussed his problems with us. "The more we do for you," Harris told him, "the less you appreciate us. So we are selling your car." Then Glenn asked if he could have his dog , a beautiful white shih tzu with a little bit of black around his nose. I had taken Bo Bey to obedience school, where he had been well-trained, and I had just had him groomed. Glenn took the dog and said goodbye. This was in February 1972. We didn't see Glenn again until 1981.

Harris' muscular dystrophy started to progress more quickly after that, and I worried about him climbing stairs. The doctor told him he would have to use two canes. I thought I was going to have a nervous breakdown worrying about the nursery, the beauty shop, Harris, and Glenn. I went to the doctor, and he gave me nerve pills and advised me to sell everything and move to Florida.

I took some time off and went to Florida, where I found a beautiful duplex on the waterway in Fort Lauderdale. I knew that Harris liked to fish and crab, and this was an ideal place. I went back to Baltimore, and we sold the house and businesses, furniture and all.

After a month in Florida, we received a letter from Glenn. He told us how sorry he was for treating us the way he did. He'd gotten our address from his aunt in Towson. He also asked us for one more favor: Would we please send him $250? He said that he missed and loved us, and that he was moving to New York. My heart melted and I cried. Just hearing from him made me happy. I sent him a check and told him that this was definitely the last time I would give him

money. Over the next nine years, our only contact with him consisted of a few postcards saying that he missed us and loved us and was well.

We missed him and prayed for him to be happy and successful. Little did we know that Glenn was quickly becoming a worldwide celebrity.

This celebrity was helped in large part by the then-fledgling film distribution company, New Line Cinema. "New Line Cinema got started over 30 years ago as a distributor of films to college campuses," remembers its founder and president, Robert Shaye. "The idea that New Line had was to create a program. So usually there were two short films, a feature film, and program notes, posters, trailers, and stuff like that. So we tried to help create an event for campus organizations.

"I first heard from John when he sent me a 16-millimeter film (*Pink Flamingos*) in one of those little fiberboard containers that films used to come in. We had an office above Smith's Bar and Grill on University Place in Greenwich Village, so it wasn't as auspicious as John probably thought it was when he sent the film to me.

"We had a putative screening room, which was really a storage area with a screen set up on a tripod and a 16-millimeter projector, and I remember putting the film on the projector and running it, and being totally mind-boggled by it. And then when we got to that one scene that you must remember if you've seen the film where there is a good-looking girl, and she pulls up her skirt and she has a penis. And when I saw that, I actually stopped the projector and rolled the film back, and I knew we had something that was appropriate for our distribution company.

"Ben Barenholtz, who was managing the Elgin Theater in New York at that time, was having a very significant success, at least in little micro-independent terms, with *El Topo*, and he had started, or was letting flourish, a very vibrant midnight-movie scene. John really was the one who suggested that Ben had seen *Pink Flamingos* and would be interested in running it at midnight. Ben and I were acquainted with each other, and we struck a deal to start showing Pink Flamingos at midnight, and it worked."

Barenholtz says, "I just thought it was a perfect film for that kind of exposure. We opened it just Friday and Saturday at midnight, and I think it did quite well for about six months, and then it started dropping off, and I decided with the New Line people to keep it running one night a week at midnight and just nurse that. And then it started picking up again."

John and Glenn's friend Bob Adams remembers going up to New York to see the film: "I remember Edith Massey, the Egg Lady from the film, standing in the freezing cold outside the Elgin grabbing people on the street and saying 'Come on in, hon. We're all in a MEW-vay.' There was nobody

there. The next week, there were lines around the block. Go figure."

Barenholtz says, "The initial audience was sort of downtown gay people, more of the hipper set, and then it started broadening. Actually, it started bringing in some of the bridge-and-tunnel crowd: working-class kids from New Jersey who would become a little rowdy."

Shaye remembers it well: "It was a real kind of New York late-night crowd. It was a crowd that, you know, stayed up until 3 or 4 o'clock in the morning, and that was used to going to the Electric Circus one night and the Elgin another. It was very exciting to see them because they almost were like people praying in some mosque or synagogue or something. They would stand up in the middle of the theater and sort of rock back and forth reciting the lines from the film, much the same way that *The Rocky Horror Picture Show* worked. The script itself became a kind of mantra that people got a big kick out of yelling back at the screen."

"People loved it. People still do," Glenn said in a 1974 interview. "I have met people who have seen it up to 32 times! You know, I think that I'm the only person who's ever seen it who has only seen it just four times. In Philadelphia once, people sat and repeated every word of dialogue—everybody's part through the whole movie. They knew it, a couple hundred of them, 'yip-yip-yip-yip-yip' all the way through the film."

Variety hated the film, calling it "surely

one of the most vile, stupid, and repulsive films ever made," but agreed that seeing it was an event. "Midnight screenings of the poorly lensed 16-millimeter picture, populated by nightcrawling ephemerids and camp following sophisticates, confer a special status on the audience. Shrill laughter and knowing hoots greet excesses, and 'in-ness,' now painstakingly sought by large segments of the hip masses, is achieved. Hence its phenomenal appeal."

Baltimore theater and film critic and radio personality Don Walls looks back on

Pink Flamingos from his perspective today. "Variety called John's cast 'the dregs of human perversity' and, although I don't want to call them freaks, they were strange people, and they couldn't read lines. They couldn't read dialogue, and it sort of made his films seem very amateurish. But I think that Divine appearing in it gave it a certain madness that made it entertaining, as opposed to some of the other people that John used in the film who were just sort of eccentric, but not really that interesting. There was something about Divine, even then, a quality of

Edith Massey as "Edie the Egg Lady" in John Waters' Pink Flamingos, *1972*

"Divine is probably one of the central drag personae of the 20th doing drag, just slapping it together and doing it."

acting that was going on the screen that didn't seem to exist in the other people John used in his films."

Glenn Belverio, who has acted in many movies and videos under the name Glenda Orgasm (no kidding!) told me that it is almost impossible to describe the huge influence Glenn's work had on other cross-dressing performers. Glenn (or Glenda) says that seeing *Pink Flamingos* for the first time was a revelation for him: "When I first saw that movie, I was genuinely shocked. I love thinking back to that time, because now I'm a jaded old lady and nothing shocks me. But back then, I just thought, *Oh, my God—this movie is really over the top.*

"The scene where Divine is walking down the street and Little Richard's 'The Girl Can't Help It' is playing on the soundtrack just left me speechless. Just the images of Divine walking down an ordinary street in Baltimore and the reaction shots of these people looking at this strange creature had such an effect on me. It made me realize what I wanted to do as an artist, that I wanted to capture the sensibility of seeing a drag queen in an unlikely situation.

"This was the basis for some of the video and performance work I have done, like taking my drag performances out onto the street, on public access cable, and even to the Empire State Building. Divine and *Pink Flamingos* were the major inspiration for all of us.

"Here in the new millennium, it's hard to remember what an amazing experience those early Divine films were when they first came out. They appeared right after the psychedelic '60s and the Warhol films with drag queens like Jackie Curtis, Holly Woodlawn, and Candy Darling. But there were just no other movies anything like *Pink Flamingos*. I think what was great was that the sensibility was very gay, but John never came out and said that this was a gay movie, and Divine never came out and said, 'I'm a drag queen.' That Divine was playing a woman's role in these movies was never questioned.

"Also, the early Waters and Divine films clearly were prophetic in that they predicted and predated the punk movement by several years. *Pink Flamingos* was released in 1972, and the whole attitude of the film is very punk. It's just kind of like, 'Fuck you, I'm in drag, I'm going to eat dog shit.' And at the end of the film, Divine and her family are talking about moving to Idaho and getting Mohawk hairdos. The elements of punk style—the energy and sensibility—were very much there. Remember, this is four years before the first Ramones album came out, which is when a lot of people say that punk started. So Divine and *Pink Flamingos* were this major cultural shift, not just in drag but in pop culture generally.

"Divine is probably one of the central drag personae of the 20th century. She really brought out the whole idea of people just doing drag, just slapping it together and doing it. Or so it seemed—we now know how hard John, Divine, and Van Smith

century. She really brought out the whole idea of people just

worked in creating the Divine character. I would never have started doing drag if it hadn't been for Divine, and when I talk to other drag queens, they always say, 'Oh, yeah. *Pink Flamingos* has had such an effect on all of our lives."

While all of this was going on in Baltimore and New York, Harris and I were settling down into retirement. We prayed for Glenn every day and thought about him all the time. It seemed like every time I turned on the TV or picked up a magazine, there was something about gay people and the problems they faced. This was a total shock to me. For years, I had felt alone when I overheard people saying such horrible and hateful things about gay people. Now gay characters were appearing on sitcoms. Archie Bunker on *All in the Family,* the top-rated show in the country, had to face the fact that one of his best friends from the local bar, a macho ex-football player named Steve, was gay. The same season, *Marcus Welby, M.D.* showed an episode about a man suffering stress because he was in the closet and leading a double life. There was even a TV movie, *That Certain Summer,* in which Hal Holbrook played a gay man who had to face the challenge of explaining his homosexuality to his teenage son. Martin Sheen played his lover, and Hope Lange was his ex-wife. The movie got great reviews and

was widely watched. Still, it was a very sad story, and it seemed to hint that gay people would have a terrible time finding happiness. And then there was a story on the half-hour drama *Room 222* about a sensitive, intelligent, and creative teenage boy who was outcast from his classmates and called "fag" for liking painting and Shakespeare. At one point he was thrown against his locker by one of the football players who says, "Come on, hit me back, fag." It brought back a lot of awful memories, and it helped me realize that there were lots of young kids facing the same troubles Glenn had faced.

I missed Glenn terribly in those first days in Florida. It was hard trying to get used to life without him. And we had worked hard for so many years at the nursery that it was difficult for us to be retired. Thankfully, the neighbors, another retired couple, enjoyed our company, and after socializing with them a lot, we really began to settle in. Harris had always enjoyed fishing, and now he could spend as much time as he wanted at the water with our new friends while doing what he loved and enjoying the warm weather.

I was restless, though, and after six months in Florida, I decided to go back to work. I got a job at Univis Optical. My job was to look at the lenses coming off the assembly line with a huge magnifying glass. I enjoyed my work, mostly because of the friends I made there, and it was only a 10-minute ride from home. It sure was a far cry from the midnight shift at Black and Decker during the early years when Harris and I were struggling to start a family.

Still, I worried a lot. I can remember sitting at work at the factory anxiously looking at the clock, waiting for my next break so I could call and check on Harris. And what about Glenn? Was he all right? I used to lie awake at night, long after Harris was asleep, and look up at the ceiling, praying to the Lord to watch over my family and me. And when I finally did drift off to sleep, I would wake up with knots in my stomach and a terrible thirst that wouldn't go away no matter how many glasses of water I drank.

I didn't want Harris to worry, so I tried not to complain, but eventually I ended up in the doctor's office. He told me I was suffering from stress-induced ulcers again, and he put me on a bland diet and in the hospital for further treatment. While I was in there, one of my friends looked after Harris. But the sleepless nights continued. I was still thinking about Glenn. It was the farthest thing from my mind that he was back in Baltimore making yet another movie with John.

That movie was *Female Trouble,* considered by many to be the best of John's early work. *Female Trouble* is the story of a teenage girl, Dawn Davenport, played by Divine, who runs away from home when she finds 'sensible shoes' under the Christmas tree instead of the cha-cha heels she wanted. After running away, she is raped by a lowlife (also played by Glenn in a body-double sequence), gets pregnant, and enters a life of

crime before being executed in the electric chair.

"The first time I met Divine," says *Female Trouble* cameraman David Insley, "I was still at University of Maryland at Baltimore County, where Leroy Morais had started the area's first film department. I was a teaching assistant for him, and John had come to him and said, 'Could you help me make this next movie?' Leroy said, 'Sure, we'd love to help. It would be a great experience for the students.' This was how we got involved in the shooting of *Female Trouble.*

"The first shoot day was Divine as a guy, Earl Peterson, the lowlife brute who rapes Dawn early in the film. So here is Divine, out of drag, grinding things and welding things in Vince Peranio's brother's shop in Fell's Point. He'd let a couple of days' beard grow, and he was wearing this stained T-shirt and work gloves. Here was this incredibly shy man quietly waiting for directions from John, and as soon as the camera would roll he would mutate into this gravelly-voiced, foul-mouthed, bigoted scumbag. I'd never seen anything like this before in my life, you know. I was the naive suburban kid, and this was just so much fun. We couldn't wait to go back and shoot all the other days. Who cares if we got paid. We were just having a great time.

"We worked in the house of Pat Moran, John's associate producer and longtime friend. That was the main set for all the interiors of Divine's house, with the birdcage

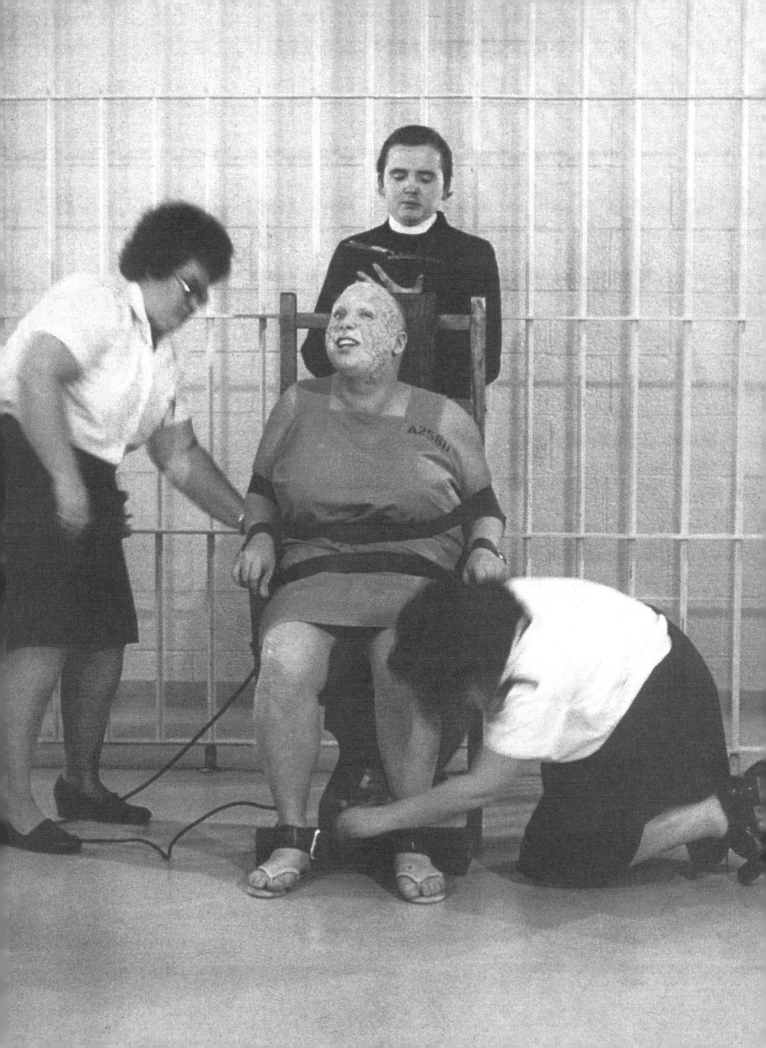

"It takes an hour and a half to make up Divine."

where Edith Massey is kept by Divine after she amputates her hands and replaces them with hooks. Leroy's two daughters would be on the set, and when we weren't shooting or rehearsing, Divine would be over there with them, singing songs and playing games. They really loved him.

"Divine and John were the big reasons to do the movies. They were just so much fun to be with—the banter and the rapport they had. It was so much fun to just listen to them. I thought Divine really became a good actor—actress, actor, whatever."

Pink Flamingos had been filmed with a newsreel camera, so there were no cutaway shots. *Female Trouble*, though, was shot double system, in which sound is recorded on a separate tape track in sync with the visuals. Clapping the slate at the beginning of each take signals starting the synchronous motor that runs both the sound and visual tracks. Glenn loved the slate-clapping.

Glenn told an interviewer on the set of *Female Trouble*, "I always wanted to work with one of them [a slate] because whenever you see films on films and they show people making movies, they use one. I always thought they were nice, when in reality when they slap that fucking thing it hurts your ears it's so loud. But that was fun, working with that, and the crew was really nice to work with. They knew what they were doing."

Glenn later told a documentary filmmaker that the long hours in makeup during *Female Trouble* were "the worst part, espe-

cially the scars and everything because that was liquid rubber, which just completely burned my face. It seemed like I lost a whole layer of skin each time. And applying the liquid rubber took a couple of hours before we even got ready to film. I would come here at 5 in the morning or earlier with Van Smith and we'd just be here by ourselves, just for my makeup alone. So that was probably the most grueling. Fittings were hard too: Costume fittings took forever."

Makeup artist Van Smith spoke with Steve Yeager on the set of *Female Trouble*: "There's so much makeup. It takes an hour and a half to make up Divine. Certain incidents and actions in the movie cause it to wipe off, or, you know, it has to be restored. She sweats a great deal, so it runs off. One time we didn't have time, so she just slept in it, and the next morning it was still fresh. I'd put it on so thick, it just sort of stuck there. Sometimes I'd wrap her face in toilet paper."

Van also acknowledged the difficulty of dressing Glenn for the day's shooting. "Fur is more expensive because it needs to be fitted right on her and all that stuff. She needs a seamstress. She can't use a pattern, of course. With fabrics you can only use stretch."

Glenn said, "I'd wake up in the morning and have no idea how long the day would be. I would think some scenes were going to take 15 minutes and they'd end up taking forever. The wedding scene, where I marry Gator, Edith Massey's nephew—that took five hours, and all I had to do was walk down the aisle. We filmed one day from 9:00 in the morning until 1:30 at night without any breaks. People think it's really glamorous, that you just sit around and look pretty and say lines, but it's really hard work."

Glenn was proud of his role in the movie, especially his male role as Earl Peterson. He thought it was more challenging than his earlier roles. "I don't want to be typecast," he said in 1974. "One thing I was very glad about was that I didn't play 'Lady Divine' in *Female Trouble*. People start believing that actually is me! That's why I've had people ask me in interviews and things if I really go around scarfing up piles of dog shit off the street and murdering people. If I ran around murdering people and eating dog shit, they'd put me away. The good thing about playing the part of Dawn Davenport was that it wasn't me at all. There is no way I can defend her. She was a hideous person."

One of Glenn's biggest fans was underground filmmaker George Kuchar, whose 1966 movie *Hold Me While I'm Naked* was a huge influence on John Waters. Kuchar sympathizes with Glenn's annoyance at some of the interview questions. "I've seen Divine on talk shows and, to me, what was most horrible and obscene was the people who were interviewing him. They were so much more twisted than he could ever be. The real sickos in our society can be found hosting morning talk shows, not in John Waters movies."

John claims he based *Female Trouble* on Glenn's high school friend, Carol Wernig, saying, "She looked just like Dawn Davenport in the beginning of *Female Trouble*. She had the same hairdo as Dawn in the beginning of the movie, except it was bleached white, but it had turned green from the chlorine in swimming pools. And she wore short shorts and had mosquito bites all over her legs. And when I first saw her I thought, 'Ooh, I've got to meet her, right?' So, as always, I exaggerated it in my mind and it became a criminal biography of Dawn Davenport played by Divine: from high school suburban skank to her death in the electric chair."

The hair designer for *Female Trouble* was Christine Mason, who later worked on *Desperate Living*, *Polyester*, and *Hairspray*. Christine became good friends with Glenn. She told me, "I was good friends with Pat Moran, and they were shooting down on Read Street near her husband's store, and it got to be like a family affair. Everyone just got up at five in the morning and showed up. Doing hair was what I did, so I just kind of jumped in and grabbed a rattail comb and a can of hairspray and sat Divine down in the chair with a wig, and away we went. We had all grown up in Baltimore in the early '60s, so we didn't have to do any research for the hairstyles. Basically, the hair just needed to be big and wide. Big and wide, that was it.

"Divine and I developed a friendship off the set. We used to pretend that he was

Elizabeth Taylor and I was Maurice the French faggot hairdresser, and we would play in those little roles for a while. We had our best relationship in California. We were living in San Francisco, and we hung out with the Cockettes, the drag queen chorus line who used to do shows at the Palace Theater.

"I think that Divine's importance in John's films, his early films in particular, was paramount. Even though John really wasn't on film, they were like a Lucy-and-Ethel kind of team together. John could act out exactly what he wanted Divine to do, and then Divine could exactly do it but in a bigger and more flamboyant fashion.

"Divine never considered himself to be a drag queen. He looked at himself as an actor, and I agree with that. I think that drag queens in particular have this idea of what women are supposed to look like. And Divine never actually looked like a woman. Sorry, Div, but you really never looked like a woman."

Makeup artist and costume designer Van Smith, who designed the whole Divine look with Glenn and John, remembers collaborating on makeup and costumes for Glenn. "John wanted this really trashy, slutty look. I would bring ideas to him, and he would say yes or no. I drew lots of sketches, and we would talk about what we wanted Divy to look like. The whole thing was highly orchestrated by John. It was John's idea to shave Divy's head, not mine. I've always been convinced that that came from the famous gag

photo of Marilyn Monroe with the Chairman Mao hairdo. Also, I was working in fashion at the time. If you go back to the '60s and look, the models wore lots of makeup, particularly around the eyes.

"John and I both considered Divy beautiful. The costuming was to be as revealing as possible. We always talked about fat as sexy. It was all to be as voluptuous as possible, as racy as possible. But Divine was political in a sense, of course, because of the exaggerated femininity in the emphasis on the breasts and hips and so forth, along with the character always having this masculine criminal drive. So on one level, Divine really was virtually beyond gender.

"When we started working together, drag was just coming onto the scene in the mainstream. In 1972 when we did *Pink Flamingos*, Paul Morrissey and Warhol did *Women in Revolt* with Candy Darling and Jackie Curtis, but they were giving a lot of 'real girl,' as the saying goes. Ours was a much more in-your-face kind of drag. It wasn't Miss Maryland. It wasn't trying to pass for a really pretty girl or anything. It was very aggressive. Divine definitely took on a larger-than-life presence, and he certainly made a later figure like RuPaul possible."

Pat Moran says, "Believe me, there wasn't a self-respecting drag queen from here to San Francisco that wanted anything to do with that look. Divine was a terrorist, a drag terrorist."

John Waters agrees. "I wanted him to be

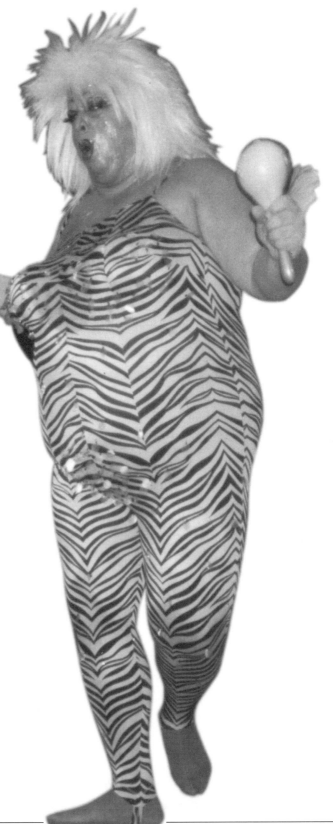

the Godzilla of drag queens. I mean, at the end of *Multiple Maniacs,* the National Guard shoots him. How much closer to Godzilla can you be? And the other drag queens were so square then. They wanted to be Miss America. Those were their values, and they hated Divine.

"In the early '70s, after Van was on board and the new, more outrageous look was underway, Divine and I used to go to these drag balls in Washington that were really frightening. They were usually all black, with pimps and people with guns and everything. I thought, *God, this is wild.* They were totally illegal. There were drugs, and the cops would raid them, and people would be running. It was fun, I'm telling you. And that's where Divine first started to put stuff in that other drag queens were frightened of.

"Being fat—first of all, there were no fat drag queens. And if there were, they didn't come with their stomach exposed, hanging out in a peekaboo look, which was Van Smith's influence. And when we got to California, Van got even more carried away. He would use fake scars a lot, and Divine would come in with weapons. I always liked to give Divine some kind of weapon to carry, where other drag queens would always carry a purse. Divine would have a purse, but there would be a machete inside, you know. And I used to write speeches for

Divine to scare hippies where he would say, 'I watched two hippie couples, and I followed them to their apartment, and then I killed their pets.'"

So, as you can see, there was a lot more to Divine than 300 pounds and a fishnet gown. In interviews, Glenn always emphasized the hard work that went into making the movies and stage appearances. And he insisted that he be taken seriously as an actor, no matter how crazy his behavior onscreen and onstage. He was very dedicated to his craft. "I don't like to watch myself onscreen," he told an interviewer in 1974. "I can see all these little things that nobody else sees, things I could have done differently." He even was serious about promotions and personal appearances. "As far as appearances go and things like that, I feel that audiences want to see me a certain way, projecting a certain image. And the certain image that I project takes hard work and money. Before I can walk out onto a stage or into the lobby of a theater, I've spent a couple of hours and almost $200. I notice I get what people have referred to as the star treatment, though, which is really nice. It's like payment: It makes all the hard work and everything worthwhile. In a way, it's better than somebody handing you a lot of money. You know you have made these people really happy, and that's mainly why I do it. And to make myself happy. When I was a child, I wanted to be a movie star. So now I have been given the chance to be a movie star, an actor—whatever you want to

call it. I feel that I am an actor. I play a woman, and people believe it. A lot of people believe that I am a woman! I'm a 28-year-old man who weighs 250 pounds that can go out and convince people he's a woman. I think that's some fine acting."

Laurence Kardish of the Museum of Modern Art, who showed *Pink Flamingos* as part of an American film comedy series, is one of many who have praised Glenn's acting and how it worked in the movie. "Transvestitism," says Kardish, "is one of the oldest comic traditions, going back to Roman and Greek theater, Shakespeare's plays, and a long tradition of live cabaret performance. One of the most striking aspects about John's films in terms of their use of transvestitism is that Divine is never explained. In a movie like *Some Like It Hot,* which I understand Glenn loved as a teenager, they use the cross-dressing idea hilariously, with Tony Curtis and Jack Lemmon dressed up as women to escape from the gangsters who are trying to kill them. Divine, though, is just a given. It's never explained. There's no good narrative reason why Glenn should be Divine. Divine just is, so you have to accept this apparition at face value."

Pat Moran, who won an Emmy for casting the Baltimore-based TV series *Homicide,* says, "John's dialogue and Divine's performance in *Pink Flamingos, Female Trouble, Hairspray*—all the films—were perfectly matched to each other. And Divine was, believe me, the ultimate actor. I mean, he's a director's dreamboat because he never ever complained. He always was prepared. He never had a better idea. The Christmas tree scene in *Female Trouble* where Dawn pulls down the tree on top of her mother because she doesn't get her cha-cha heels is a great example. I mean, Divine loved Christmas so much, so to do that scene must have seemed odd to him, but he was totally in the service of John's vision."

"The Christmas tree scene in *Female Trouble* happened in real life, sort of, when I was very young," says John. "The Christmas tree fell over on my grandmother. I wasn't there. I heard about it, and she wasn't pinned under it or anything, but I exaggerated it in my mind always. My parents have told me that when my grandmother was fixing the tree and decorating it, it fell over on her. I was obsessed by that as a child. I said, 'Were the presents injured?'"

If the Christmas tree scene was traumatic for Glenn, the prison scene must have been even more difficult.

"I remember when we actually filmed that scene from *Female Trouble* in the Baltimore City Jail," says John. "We showed up that morning and there had been a riot, and the warden, Gordon Kamka, still let us go in, which [made us feel] a little uneasy. So there we were, carrying this prop electric chair through the yard of the prison when, don't forget, capital punishment was illegal. So all the prisoners were yelling and cussing at us out the window, 'What the hell is this?

They're bringing this in?' And Divine was very frightened going in that prison because he had been in the jail two years before, when we were making *Pink Flamingos,* for writing bad checks. He couldn't believe that I had gotten permission to film in the city jail when he had been in there as an inmate.

"So we got the scene set up to shoot the electrocution, and he was sitting in the electric chair. He always thought I somehow was going to give him a shock for the performance, and I kept saying, 'I promise you. Look, it's not hooked into anything!' He was really suspicious of everything that day. But he'd had to stroll through the prison, in drag with a shaved head with thick scars all over his face, carrying an electric chair. I guess that is an uncomfortably high-profile way to enter a penitentiary.

"*Female Trouble* is my favorite of all of my earlier films. It's the ultimate Divine vehicle. It just proved what a great star Divine was.

"I had outrageous physical things in the movie, too, to prove that we were insane to do this kind of thing, that we would never use a stunt double or special effects. Divine did swim the rapids, and it was in November. The water was quite cold, and rapids are hard to swim. It was part of the scariness of the movie to real people that here was a man playing a woman who would leap into the rapids of a river and do a stunt in drag.

"The same with the trampoline in the nightclub scene. I got Divine lessons at the YMCA near where I lived, and the instructor,

84

"I just spend a lot of time at the beach and going to Hollywood a
around. I like to eat, get high, get dirty. That's about all. When I'n

Mr. Caster, didn't know anything about a movie or Divine being in drag or anything. He just had to teach him how to do a flip.

"Mr. Caster showed up the day we shot the scene and saw Divine in full drag and just started laughing. He was just a really good sport, standing there with Divine, patiently instructing, 'One, two, three, flip. One, two, three, flip.' It was a lot harder to do in drag because he had all this stuff on him, wigs and everything. I remember Divine was very relieved when we got that take because he feared for his physical safety. He weighed 300 pounds at the time. But he went to his lessons and learned how to do it, and when it was time to shoot, he was ready and did it with great skill, I think."

Glenn was very proud of his work on *Female Trouble,* and as the film was being completed, he talked about his hard work to an interviewer in Baltimore: "As a movie goes through various stages of planning, John will think of other things he wants you to do for that particular character. Some of the things he thought of, like swimming that river—that was a frightening experience. Just look at the way the current was moving. I got to the location, I was wearing all this makeup and costume padding and I thought, *Well, there's no turning back now.* I told him I would do it, and I wanted to please him. And of course I want to please myself, you know. And if I had said, 'No,' I'm sure he would never have forced me to jump into the river. But I would have disappointed him, I

would have disappointed the people who came to the movie, and I would have disappointed myself. So I jumped into the river and swam across, and with the current, I could feel it carrying me down. I just swam a little harder to get to the other side.

"Now, the trampoline—that scared the shit out of me. John got me lessons, and the first couple of times I went, it was all right. I mean, I'm not a very physical person. I like swimming, and I ride and things, but that's as far as I go. But, like in school when they make you climb those ropes and all that kind of stuff, I was never any good at any of that. So here I was, doing something that I said I'd do. The first couple of times it was all right, and then I fell through the springs. I almost fell off and cut my legs all up. That freaked me out. So the next time I went, I was starting to do that backflip, and I fell on my face. That's when I did not want to go back at all. It was very scary, and I was very glad when that scene was over."

Reviews of *Female Trouble* were mixed. *Variety* said, "Film purists, establishment critics, and ordinary folks will shudder.... The costumes alone, credited to Van Smith, give new meaning to vulgarity, making some Frederick's of Hollywood creations look like items from Sears Roebuck." *The Village Voice,* however, loved it. "Opening night [at the Elgin] was a smash," Glenn O'Brien wrote in March 1975. "Hundreds more than would fit in the theatre showed up. Divine rolled up in a limo. Dressed all in gold, she cut through the teem-

Baby Glenn's first portrait

Glenn's 5th birthday

Top left: Glenny's bronzed booties
Below: Diana Evans with Glenn dressed as Elizabeth Taylor on Halloween, 1963

This page, clockwise from top left:
Richard Bernstein and Glenn on the
Metroliner to Washington for the
premiere of *Women Behind Bars*

Live performance in Mexico.

Interview cover painted and designed by
Richard Bernstein

Opposite page, clockwise from top left:
Patriotic Divine

Poster for *Neon Woman* designed and
painted by Richard Bernstein

Fashion shoot at Vincent Nasso's

Lust in the Dust director Paul Bartel giving
Divine the ride of his life

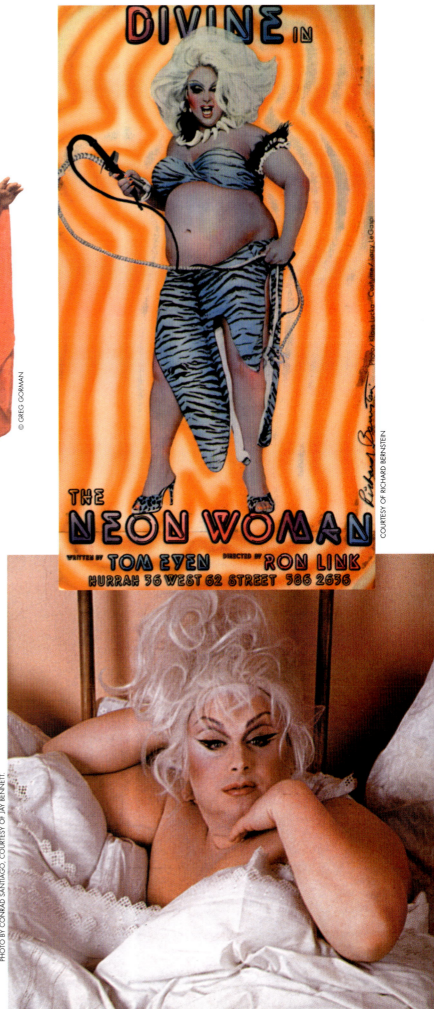

DIVINE IN

THE NEON WOMAN

WRITTEN BY **TOM EYEN**   DIRECTED BY **RON LINK**

HURRAH 36 WEST 62 STREET 586 2636

Aunt Doris, Aunt Wanda, Frances, Carmen, Glenn, Oscar, and Harris

Glenn and Zandra Rhodes at Christmas

New Year's at the Glass House with Andrew Logan. Divy adorned with Andrew's jewels

Divine in London, 1981

Lee L'Ecuyer and Glenn at the after-party for the opening of Polyester

John Waters and Divine outside the Senator Theatre at the premiere of Hairspray *in Baltimore*

Frances and Glenn at the after-party for Hairspray

John Waters, Pat Moran, and Glenn at the premiere of Hairspray

Glenn as the distinguished gentleman

Next page:
The ultimate glamour shot of Divine

ight.   I really don't do anything. I'm a slob. I just like to sit
ot working, I like to do nothing."

ing fans like a hot knife through oleo, shakin'
and shimmyin' and sashayin'. She was a hit.
But John looked like he was worrying a bit,
wondering if he should be here uptown. It
had taken months for *Flamingos* to build to
this hysteria. But tonight they were rolling in
the aisles."

By this time, Glenn had left Baltimore
and taken up residence in Santa Monica,
California. His expensive tastes had not
changed, though. "It's a real nice house," he
told interviewer and filmmaker Steve Yeager.
"It has a gate on the street that goes back.
It's about 200 feet off the street, and the
walkway is just completely covered with vines
and things. It's sort of Mexican, because you
walk up onto a porch, and then there are
these little adobe steps that go up to a roof
garden that overlooks the ocean. And then
there's a skylight, and then you go back
down the stairs to the living room. There's a
sitting room, a hallway, and my bedroom. To
get to my bedroom, you just walk down the
steps. It's just open all the way—I don't have
any doors or anything. Then I have a lanai,
which is a closed-in patio, and the top is all
covered in vines, and then there's a little
guest house, and that's it: my humble abode.

"I just spend a lot of time at the beach
and going to Hollywood at night. I really
don't do anything. I'm a slob. I just like to sit
around. I like to eat, get high, get dirty.

That's about all. When I'm not working, I like
to do nothing. That's not true, really, I love to
watch movies. They're the only things I watch
on television—the news and the movies. I go
to a lot of movies, too. I like Russ Meyer's
movies. John likes them a lot too. They're
really good."

After a couple of years in Florida, I
decided Harris and I needed to move away
from the waterway for Harris's protection.
We moved into a beautiful Spanish-style
three-bedroom home, white with yellow trim,
in Oakland Hills in Margate. The house had
a sunken living room and a family room
overlooking the outside. There was a gated
and arched front entrance. It was a beautiful
house for a family, but our family was incom-
plete. We missed Glenn and hoped that he
was happy and had people in his life who
loved and cared for him.

I learned later that this was the case. John
and Glenn's friend Chuck Yeaton, who is
also Pat Moran's husband, says, "Divine is our
son Brook's godfather, and that was a very
unusual and very unique relationship. It started out at a very young and tender age for
Brook. Here you have a 5- or 6-year-old boy
who happens to have a 300-pound person
in his life that is feminine to a certain extent,
although Divine was never in drag per se, or
in costume or makeup, when he was socially
involved with us. But Brook was on the set for

PHOTOS BY STEVE YEAGER. © 1998 FRAME ENLARGEMENTS FROM STEVE YEAGER'S
DOCUMENTARY *DIVINE TRASH*, 1998.

a number of the films and saw Divine in his outrageous outfits. For some reason the two of them just became very close. I would say their bond was as strong as Brook's bond is with his mother and me. Brook took it very hard when Div passed away. But it was quite unique, and it was a joy and a pleasure to have him as a part of lives."

Brook remembers it this way: "My mother, Pat Moran, was casting director for all of John Waters's films, so I was surrounded by John and Divy for as long as I can remember. It was never hard for me or any of my family members to differentiate, if you will, Divine performing and Divine offstage, because I always knew him as someone who worked on films. In fact, I thought that every family made a film in the summer. It's just the way I was raised. I thought that every year, every family made a movie."

In his comments to interviewers and fans, Glenn nearly always came across as a very shy and private person—a far cry from the crazy characters he used to play in John's movies. Much of this, he later told me, had to do with his desire to protect his privacy and to keep Harris and me from finding out what he was doing before he had something he knew he could share with us.

Still, he worked very hard to promote the movies and to branch out into music and theater. How he thought he could become as big a star as Elizabeth Taylor and protect his identity at the same time is beyond me.

After *Female Trouble* was released, Glenn continued his personal appearances, which were usually based on material written by John, at places like the Palace Theater in San Francisco and the Theater of the Living Arts in Philadelphia. In Philadelphia, they had Glenn pop out of a cake and dance around the stage waving plastic pink flamingos on a stick. He would often recite the crazy monologue from the nightclub scene in *Female Trouble*. And he always harassed the audience with outrageous jokes. So, basically his stage act was an X-rated version of the way he'd joked with customers at the beauty salons he'd worked at: No matter how cutting his jokes were, he'd bat his gorgeous blue eyes and everyone, including the person he was joking on, would burst out laughing.

After *Female Trouble* was released, Glenn told an interviewer, "I really love working with John, and I want to continue working with him. But I do want to work with other directors too. I want to experience all

that, because I like meeting different people and meeting people that I don't know and making new friends and acquaintances. It's pretty easy working with John and all of his people...because I've known them all so long. I know all their faults, I know all their good points, and, you know, they all know mine. I think when you're working with people and you're thrown together the way we all have been on movies like *Pink Flamingos* and *Female Trouble,* if you didn't know these people, it would be more of a strain on you because you have to go through all of those things, getting used to different personality traits and all that.

"Plus, I love the stories and ideas that John comes up with. He refers to his movies as trash epics and things like that, but when people ask me what kind of movies I make, I always refer to them as comedies. I think they're extremely funny. But I have other people that disagree, that think his movies are just really sick—sick movies, sick people. But they're not—they're just to entertain. Sometimes, I've been offered other scripts, and I try to read them, and they just seem like they're missing something."

"Well, you should get out more. Bachelor cotillions, parties, country clubs. I've been on top of the world lately with my debutante party coming up. I've already rented the hall, Francine. It will be a beautiful affair. Every little detail will be perfect."

—Cuddles (Edith Massey), *Polyester* (1981)

After *Female Trouble,* Glenn did not work with John Waters for another six years. In 1976, Glenn was cast in an off-Broadway play, *Women Behind Bars,* written by Tom Eyen, which opened at the Truck and Warehouse Theater. Glenn played the scheming head of a women's prison. His role, Pauline, had a lot of the loudmouthed hysterical craziness of the characters he (and others) had played in John's films, and reviewers singled him out for praise. It was during this New York run of *Women Behind Bars* that Bernard Jay first encountered Glenn. (Bernard later became Glenn's manager.) The play was a big success in New York, and Glenn's contract was extended into 1977, which conflicted with the filming of John Waters's next movie, *Desperate Living.*

John remembers: "It was in the winter of 1976-77 that I had written the script and secured financing for *Desperate Living.* Divine was doing *Women Behind Bars,* and he had a contract. Of course, I wanted Divine to be in *Desperate Living.* Originally, Divine

was slated for the role of Mole McHenry, the butch lesbian who has the sex change. I thought this would be a great change from the role of Dawn Davenport and would accent his range as a performer and throw audiences for a loop. So, certainly it was putting him in a role of another character that he had never, ever played before.

"Never was Divine going to play Muffy, the femme Liz Renay part, which some people thought. Divine was always going to play the Mole part. But, of course, he couldn't. He had signed a contract for *Women Behind Bars,* and it was a hit.

"I couldn't wait six months until the play was over. When they say yes and get ready to give you the money, you make the movie before they change their mind! And I think Divine wanted to get away from me for a time, and he had a hit play that didn't have to do with me, which I certainly understand in hindsight. We weren't fighting or anything."

Because Glenn wasn't available, Susan Lowe played the part of Mole. Eventually,

"Francine Fishpaw" and Steve Yeager on the set of Polyester, *1980*

Ricki Lake and me at the Hairspray *premiere*

Women Behind Bars went on tour, and Glenn, the star, went with it.

While this was going on, my part of Florida was being splashed all over the national news. Just down I-95 about 30 miles from Margate, a local gay rights organization held a meeting with 65 political candidates in the summer of 1976 to discuss the growing lesbian and gay population of Dade County and the discrimination those individuals faced in housing and employment. After 45 of those candidates were elected—with huge support from the lesbian and gay community—the Metropolitan Dade County Commission passed an ordinance outlawing discrimination based on "affectional or sexual preferences."

What came next was bizarre. Anita Bryant, spokesperson for Florida orange juice and 1959 Miss America runner-up, led a bigoted and mean-spirited campaign to have the ordinance repealed. Her organization, Save Our Children (*What about children like mine?* I thought at the time), collected over 64,000 signatures to have the repeal of the ordinance placed on the ballot in a special summer referendum.

Anita told her followers that the law legitimized "homosexuals and their recruitment of our children." In support of her campaign, news footage showed a chubby TV preacher from Virginia whom no one had ever heard of, the Reverend Jerry Falwell, saying, "You have no idea how mean and vicious these people are. They'd just as soon kill you as

look at you."

I kept my feelings about this issue to myself, but it really offended me to hear people say such horrible things about gays. And it made me furious that these people were doing this in the name of religion.

In June, the gay rights ordinance was repealed by a margin of more than 2 to 1. When she gave her press conference to celebrate the victory, Anita kissed her husband on the lips like a prom queen at the end of a date, and he turned to the camera and said, "This is what heterosexuals do, fellows." I wanted to gag. Later, when the orange juice people fired Anita Bryant, I have to admit I was glad.

During this time, Glenn and *Women Behind Bars* traveled to London. As with many touring plays, the supporting cast was drawn from local talent. It was during the London run of *Women Behind Bars* that Glenn met the nucleus of friends who would eventually become his London family.

"Divy was a mutual friend of a fabulous designer friend of mine whom he knew from Provincetown," says fashion designer Zandra Rhodes. "We were both staying with a friend in Los Angeles, and then a few months later, he was London to do his first run of *Women Behind Bars*. So he came to London from New York with Frankie Piazza,

the dresser, and his whole group. One day he just showed up at my house and asked, 'Can I stay with you?'

"I used to take him around on the weekends, and that's when I introduced him to the group that became his extended London family—Andrew Logan the sculptor, Andrew's partner Michael Davis, Robyn Beeche the photographer, and some of the rest. He would always hold court at my house in the evenings. And of course whenever I was in the States we would get together, either at the 58th Street penthouse he shared with Jay Bennett or in Baltimore, where our favorite pastime was driving around looking at all of the estates we'd like to own.

"I saw him onstage in *Women Behind Bars* and later in *Neon Woman*. I loved him as a stage personality. There was so much more to him as a performer than was ever realized or exploited. He would have been wonderful doing one-person acts the way Bobby Short does, just sitting on the edge of a piano telling stories: *An Evening With Divine*.

"He was a superb raconteur, and he always used to tell the story about when he and Frankie and all the other fellows shared a flat on the ground floor in a huge Victorian house. They had just done a show, and Divy was dressed in his usual Chinese outfit with

Divy and Andrew Logan having tea

92

PHOTO BY KLAUS LUCKA

the little ballet shoes. So he walked into his bedroom, and there was a burglar on the floor going through his things. Divy's eyes popped wide open, and his jaw dropped to the floor. He couldn't say anything, so the guy rushed past him, and Divy screamed, 'Burglar, burglar!' and the other [roommates] caught the guy and wrestled him to the ground. They were all panicking, not knowing what to do with this guy while trying to ring the police. Eventually, the police got there, walked in, looked at the guy held on the floor, then looked over at Divy standing in the door in his makeup and earrings, and asked, 'Which one is the victim?' "

In the years since my Glenny's death, Andrew Logan and Michael Davis have been wonderful friends to me. We have remained close. Andrew recently remembered the first time he met Glenn. "It was at the Alternative Queen's Jubilee Party at my studio on Butler's Wharf. Zandra Rhodes, the fashion designer, brought by this sweet-tempered gentleman named Divine. He was fascinated by the party, which involved dressing mannequins on our balcony like the King and Queen and waving at the royals as they sailed by as part of the official Jubilee celebration.

"I next saw him in a performance of *Women Behind Bars* at the Whitehall Theater just next to Trafalgar Square. I was amazed to see what a powerful performer he was

onstage, nothing like the quiet man who had been my guest at the party.

"Divine had thought when he was booked into this theater that it was a good central place to be in order to draw a large theater crowd. In fact, the Whitehall Theater was famous for farce and soft porn. Also, the English actress he was billed with was Fiona Richmond, who was popular in soft porn films. So the audience was almost exclusively straight men in mackintoshes—what Americans call the 'raincoat crowd'—there to see Fiona Richmond naked hopping from bed to bed in a series of simulated sex scenes. And Divine was stomping around in this nurse's outfit seemingly from another planet. The men in the macs just sat there astonished. They couldn't quite believe their eyes."

After *Women Behind Bars*, Tom Eyen wrote another play, *Neon Woman*, this time with Glenn in mind. Glenn was always very proud of this project. In many ways, it was a signal to him that he was gaining respect as an actor apart from his roles in the various John Waters projects.

In my collection of Glenn's memorabilia from this time is a blurry, black-and-white

Behind the scenes in London with Zandra Rhodes

videotape of *Neon Woman* from the play's run at the Alcazar Theater in San Francisco. The play is set in Baltimore in 1962, and Glenn plays Flash Storm, the owner of a burlesque house that is being threatened by the vice squad and a hypocritical right-wing senator. When Glenn's character Flash comes onstage dressed in a huge caftan and turban and announces, "I am the Neon Woman, the original flasher, the last of the pink-hot strippers," the crowd goes bananas. The plot moves from one crazy event to another, including a series of black-stocking strangulation murders—which makes me think about the awful Sally Crough case—and an ending in which everyone is revealed to be related to everyone else.

Just as when I saw *Female Trouble,* when I play the videotape and look at Glenn in *Neon Woman,* I see little details that make me think of events and people from his life: When Flash's daughter catches her sleeping with the bouncer at the club, Glenn is dressed and made up like Marie Antoinette. The character of the senator, Horace Bradley, is a very funny version of the Southern Baptist bigots who later criticized our beloved Reverend Higgenbotham for giving the eulogy at Glenn's funeral in Baltimore. And late in the play, Flash talks about the abuse she suffered in her childhood and teenage years, and the words could almost have come from Glenn himself: "I lost my faith in mankind. That made me hate. That's why I became this overblown

Glenn's close friend and roommate Jay Bennett

cartoon for protection. No one is ever going to see the real me ever again—the thin, vulnerable little angel, instead of this big, flashy, fabulous exterior!"

Jay Bennett, who would become Glenn's close friend and roommate until the end of Glenn's life, met Glenn during *Neon Woman*'s first theatrical run in New York. "I had friends who owned the club Hurrah! in New York City, which was where the play had its first and most successful engagement," Jay told me. "I went to the club around Valentine's Day of 1978 and had a pretty menial clerical position helping out my friends. Then, one day right before the play was going to open, a local TV news crew was there to shoot Divine onstage in his full makeup for a "Talk of the Town" kind of piece on the opening of the play, and suddenly Divine stopped everything and said, 'Wait. Don't shoot anything yet. This stage is filthy, and I don't think we want to be on TV with it looking like this.' So, nobody was doing anything, so I just grabbed a broom and swept the stage. Next thing I knew I was the assistant stage manager, doing props and costumes and running the follow spot.

"At this point, right before the heyday of Studio 54, Hurrah! was the most popular club in the city, and *Neon Woman* was just about the hottest ticket in town. It had to be just about the first theatrical play ever put on in a discotheque, and there were celebrities there every night—Eartha Kitt, Elton John, and Liza Minelli would all be there sitting on cushions on the floor just like any other fan. The play was hilarious, and the audience ate it up. I wasn't really familiar with Tom Eyen's *Women Behind Bars,* but I was a huge fan of the TV soap opera parody, *Mary Hartman, Mary Hartman,* and he [Eyen] had been one of Norman Lear's writers for the show. *Neon Woman* had the same sensibility but was even more outrageous. Plus, we had a great cast of downtown underground performers in addition to Divine—Billy Edgar, also known as "Sweet William," was in the role of Flash's friend Kitty, Maria Duvall played the deaf-mute stripper, and the cast was rounded out by Brenda Bergman and Helen Hampt, who was later in a couple of Woody Allen movies. Ron Link did a great job directing, and the play was just a huge hit.

"I was a 22-year-old kid just out of drama school in Boston, and it just blew me away to be part of such an amazing show. Incredibly, I had never heard of Divine and didn't know anything about *Pink Flamingos.* But my college friends who had come down to the city with me and with whom I was sharing an apartment were always talking about 'Babs' and saying stuff like, 'Babs would love that,' and I never had any idea what they were talking about. So one day I came home and said, 'I'm working on this play, and there's this guy Divine in it,' and they were just flabbergasted. Then they told me that Babs was Divine's character in *Pink Flamingos* and that they were huge fans. Actually, soon after that our apartment broke up because they were all so jealous.

"Like most people, I guess, I was struck by the incredible dichotomy between this larger-than-life character and the cute, shy, cherubic guy with great manners I saw at rehearsal every day. He had the nicest manners of anyone I had ever seen, and he was incredibly professional, particularly in his dealings with the media. He gave great interviews, and later when we took the show on the road, he was critical in getting us coverage.

"We just hit it off and became really good friends. And when the play's first run ended sometime in the summer or fall of 1978, we moved in together into this fabu-

BORN TO BE CHEAP

lous little penthouse on 58th Street, which Zandra Rhodes would later call our 'pent-hut'. That became our home base for the next 18 months. I was on unemployment a lot, and there were times where we had to scrounge, but it was really one of the most fabulous times of my life. And no, we were never boyfriends. I was a friend, a confidante, and later a nanny to his dogs, but that was it. Still, I was closer to him than to most of the other people in my life.

"Back in those days, we lived great, but we were scrounging for money all of the time. We were always figuring out ways to open charge accounts. Or I would get [an unemployment check], and then we'd spend it all on a dinner party. I just picked up where he'd left off in the '70s with all of those stories about the things he'd done to his mother. We didn't steal, but we always wangled something. Our day-to-day life was pretty predictable: We woke up, smoked pot, and went shopping. I cooked a big dinner, and we had people over.

"At this point, Div's New York family, who he surrounded himself with just like he did with John and Pat Moran in Baltimore, was the designer Larry LeGaspi, Vincent Nasso, the dresser Frankie Piazza, and Conrad Santiago, the *Vogue* makeup artist. They're all gone now, unfortunately. We used to have a great time with them. Three

of them lived together in this fabulous apartment on 16th Street, and we'd spend weekends with them and do these crazy fashion shoots just for fun, sometimes with Divy, sometimes with models who would come by to hang out.

"This was the time of Studio 54, and there were parties every night. Div would never go to parties in drag, by the way, unless it was some sort of promotional thing. Out of drag, his look was Zandra Rhodes-designed hand-painted chiffon pants with overcoats. Also, Larry LeGaspi did some of his clothes at this time. Larry was also designing clothes for Patti LaBelle and KISS. Around the very end of the *Neon Woman* period, Tom Eyen wrote a song for Div called "Born to Be Cheap," and when Divy recorded the song and started to think about how to promote it...he would show up at some of the clubs in drag. But when he was just Divy out at a club with his friends, he was always out of drag."

One of Glenn's favorite songs, "The Name Game," was on the B side of "Born To Be Cheap." I can remember Glenn singing it with his friends in high school. It was around this time that Bernard Jay conceived of Glenn's nightclub act, designed to capitalize on the "Born To Be Cheap" single and the disco dance craze.

Also in 1978, Glenn returned to England for a number of theatrical shows and cabaret engagements. One of the highlights of this period was his appearance in the Alternative Miss World pageant, a mock beauty contest started in 1972 by Glenn's friend Andrew Logan that had become an annual event in London's high-camp fringe. Men, women, and even children dressed up in outrageous costumes and competed for the title of Alternative Miss World.

Andrew described this annual event as "a surreal art event for all-around family entertainment." He continues, "In 1978, we invited Divine to be Guest of Honor at the

Glenn with contestants of the Alternative Miss World pageant, 1978

seventh annual Alternative Miss World. I was host and hostess and wore a half-military, half-drag costume as I introduced the contestants. Also present were a range of London's fringe personalities, including my scintillating secretary Luciana and designer Zandra Rhodes as a member of the panel of judges. Contestants were judged in categories of day wear, evening wear, swimsuits, and personality.

"We filmed the 1978 pageant in luminous 35-millimeter with Richard Gayer directing. Divine appeared onstage briefly,

even though he was suffering from a severe virus and had a high fever. In the film you can see him standing backstage slump-shouldered and disoriented, but when he was announced, he hit the stage with a real energetic fury. He was a true professional.

"When the film was completed, we took it to Cannes, and Divine came with us. We were renting this fabulous chateau and having parties every night. When *Alternative Miss World* was screened, Divine attended the showing and then sneaked out the back door as soon as the film began. He didn't want to

Divy by the sea, Marbella, 1985

PHOTO BY ANNE CERSOSIMO, COURTESY OF ANNE CERSOSIMO

stay away from a wonderful party that was in progress at the chateau. He didn't go to a single movie at Cannes that year.

"The film had several different premieres in London, and Divine was on hand for all of them. For the premiere at the Odeon on Leicester Square, Divine rented a stretch limousine, and the police would not let him stop in front of the theater. So Divine went around the block a few times and finally ordered the driver to stop in front of the theater. He then leapt out and ran into the cinema.

"One of the other premieres was at the Chelsea Classic. We hired the Rothschilds' coach with four black horses. Divine was dressed in a purple gown and rode in the coach with me and Luciana. We also had an open-top bus in the entourage serving drinks. There were many future pop stars on that bus. I know Boy George was one of them."

Brook Yeaton remembers the following summer in Provincetown when *Neon Woman* was there on tour. "I was about 9 years old. He was doing *Neon Woman,* and my parents and I happened to be in town, not knowing that he was in town too. And I remember running up Commercial Street to Divy and running into his arms and having a great summer with him that year. That was one of the best summers I've ever had. I wanted to be with Div as much as I possibly could, but he had to work a couple of hours

a night. So he gave me a picture of what I now know as props. He gave me a picture of items on a table. He said at the end of the night, take all these items and put them in this box. And you're going to have to understand I was 9. And then the next day, take the picture and put the items exactly where you took them from on the prop table. So I did that for about two and a half weeks, and then about 10 years later I understood that I was actually propping—was a prop master. But that's the way John's films were and Divy was. It was always a communal effort. Everyone did everyone else's job. We just had to get it done.

"He was like my Auntie Mame, if you will. He spoiled me rotten. Anything I wanted he gave to me tenfold. Divine actually told me on many occasions that I was like his son, because he didn't believe that he would ever have a son. And if he did, of course, he would want him to be like me. That's what he told me. We had no blood relation, but we had a connection of the soul. We had a connection that was beyond family— and actually still is.

"I remember when I was graduating from high school, he said 'What would you like?' And I said, 'I'd like to see the world,' as a joke. He took me to Europe. He put me on his payroll at 18 to be his assistant sound technician, and we went to Norway, to England, to Holland, to Germany. It was wonderful. It was a wonderful time; my first tour.

"Back in Baltimore, when he was out of

drag, we'd go to Lexington Market when I was little, and people would point and laugh at his size. But Divine always told me the people who point and laugh are just doing that to make themselves feel better. They're actually very insecure. And with Divy and John and everyone in the family while I was growing up, that was the main rule. A motto that I have now is *Esse quam videri,* which is Latin for 'To be rather than to seem.' If you have a good heart and you do well and do the best at what you're doing, nothing else matters—the way you look, the way you dress, or your social or economic status really doesn't matter."

"I also met Divy during *Neon Woman,*" remembers his friend Steve Friedman. "I had been a huge fan of his, and we became fast friends for the last 13 years of his life. In fact, I lived right around the corner from him and

Jay. As someone who was first acquainted with the Divine character, I was initially surprised at what a homebody the real Divy was. Div had great dinner parties. He was a good cook, but he was a great supervisor. He knew his way around the kitchen, but he had the rest of us doing the slicing and the dicing along with the cooking and the frying and the baking. He would tell us what to do. So, in essence he was a good cook but lazy as can be. Spending the holidays with Divy, whether in New York or later in Florida with Frances and Harris, I was his 'first in command.' I would be transmitting his orders to the 'staff.' He would host dinner parties and hold court. The guests were expected to come and pay homage to him.

"He was always extremely generous during the holidays. There was no one who was overlooked or got any fewer than half a dozen presents. He loved Christmas. He would make sure the house was decorated and would coordinate all the cooking and

Carmen Fernandez, Glenn, and me

buying. Even when he was penniless, he started his holiday buying in January. There were times that he would be quite broke during the long stretches between shows. He suffered during these lean times. His lifeline, shopping, was gone, and that was pretty tough for him when he didn't have money. When he was traveling, he was constantly buying gifts for everybody. One of my favorite memories of him is shopping with complete abandon at Harrod's. The only thing better than that was to see the look on the face of his manager, Bernard Jay, when he opened up the American Express bill.

"Still, Divine was not the easiest person in the world to be friends with. He would hold court, and he was very needy. Keeping a full-time job and stopping by Divy's for a joint and lunch and then going back to work was difficult. Your time was not your own. I think he was very easily hurt. Those who were his friends and lived with his eccentricities and loved him anyway had nothing, of course, to gain materially from this."

Zandra Rhodes also remembers Glenn's love of friends and the holidays. "Christmas of 1980 was a memorable time for all of us in London. Divy was at my house that year, and Larry Hagman of TV's *Dallas* was there also. Divy would put on a red chiffon with gold embroidery that I did that looked wonderful on him, and would lay on the couch and eat chocolate as people swirled around him in constant holiday activity. He looked like Cleopatra. When it came time to deco-

rate the tree, he just lay there on the couch instructing us in that whisper-like voice of his, 'You need another blue ball up there, Zandra. Right—no, a little more to the right.'

"We all know the two things he didn't care for were early wake-ups and plastic Christmas trees, and that year I had a plastic tree, and he insisted on accompanying me to the flower market to get some decorations for the house. I warned him, 'If you want to go to the flower market, we'll have to go at 5 o'clock in the morning.' The next morning at 4 o'clock, I awoke to find him standing at the side of my bed with his chiffon and coat on, holding a cup of tea and whispering, 'Wake up! Wake up!'"

This was a very difficult time for Harris and me. I missed Glenn more than ever, and I was worried that if something happened to Harris or me, we wouldn't be able to contact him, and if something were to happen to him, we might never find out about it. Whenever I turned on the news, it seemed like

Glenn with Larry Hagman in London for Christmas

something terrible was happening to gay people. First came Anita Bryant and similar hate campaigns, then the assassination of Harvey Milk, then AIDS. I prayed every night that Glenn was healthy and all right.

As Glenn finished his extended tour of *Neon Woman* and worked on his nightclub act, John Waters prepared to shoot another movie in Baltimore. That movie was *Polyester.* It was the publicity push for *Polyester* that brought Glenn back into Harris's and my lives.

Polyester was the first of John's movies to get an R (as opposed to an X) rating, and it was the first to be shot with an honest-to-goodness crew of movie professionals. Consequently, Glenn was finally able to show his talents in a movie that mainstream audiences might see.

In the film Glenn plays Francine Fishpaw, a depressed housewife married to a jerk named Elmer, who has bought their suburban Baltimore home with the profits from his porno movie theater. Her son is a serial foot-stomping sex criminal, and her daughter is a teenage mom-to-be. "I'm having an abortion, and I can't wait!" is her most famous line. After Francine's life begins to fall apart, she has an affair with Todd Tomorrow, played by Tab Hunter (who has been an utterly wonderful person since Glenn passed away).

John Waters talked to interviewer Steve Yeager about his changing approach to film-making. "I think I learned after *Desperate Living,* which at the time did not do very well, that basically the two things regular movie-goers like least are camp and surrealism. Camp means that they don't get it and you're making fun of them. And surrealism is, 'Hey, that could never happen!'

"In *Polyester,* I was making a comedy about suburbia, so it was important to tone things down a little. The costumes and make-up were really scaled down from *Desperate Living* to *Polyester* because I wanted to make it real. My set designer Vince Peranio points out that after the movie was shot, all the ugly furniture we used was bought by the neighbors in a yard sale. So we must have gotten something right.

"I see friends of my parents that have on lime green pants with whales on them, and I think, *They think I look weird?* These, to me, are the freakish outfits. I feel like giving them some candy corn and dropping an apple in their trick-or-treat package.

"I wanted to give Divine a new kind of role. I think it broadened Divine's career in a great way to play a woman that was certainly not Divine at all—the Divine we knew from these early movies—but a real house-wife, a very believable woman. It was certainly never part of the plot of my movies that Divine was a man. But in *Polyester,* which we made in 1981, it was really less so, because

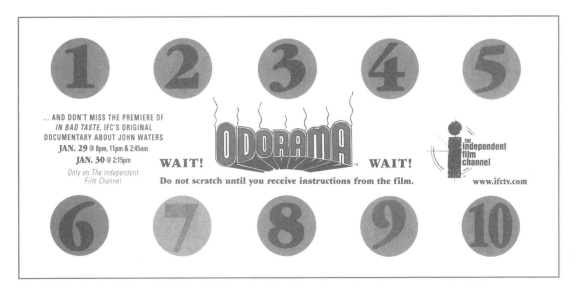

Divine was no longer a drag queen. Divine was a woman that could have been your mother, and I thought it was more subversive and scarier to have Divine branch out and play a victim. Divine had never played a victim.

"Of course, this was the movie shot in Odorama. You got a card that had numbers from 1 to 10 when you went into the theater, and when that number appeared on the screen, you scratched and sniffed that number. The smells were cued to the action in the film—smells such as gasoline, old socks, a rose, and yes, a fart. I've actually sat in the back of a theater and watched people pay me money to smell shit. I saw them. They heard a fart on the soundtrack, they saw the number flash up on the screen, and still they scratched the cards. Some of them were offended. What did they expect?

"The scratch-and-sniff card was a souvenir book to take home. Actually, we had to print up several runs of them in different languages for *Polyester*'s international release. In Mexico we had to print up a bunch of replacements at the last minute because they'd been manufactured in sweatshops and the Odorama patches had fallen off."

Glenn was very excited to be working with John again. He felt that John's movies were improving film by film and that bigger budgets wouldn't take away from their creative spark. "His whole style of moviemaking, I think, would remain the same if he had

$2 million or if he went back and made another one for $2,000," Glenn said. "I don't think it would make any difference. It would still look like a John Waters movie.

"I have worked for John for many years, and I hoped I always could. I really don't care about the money or any of that. I used to do it for nothing, and I would again, in a minute, just to work with him, because I love his style of writing and his movies.

"I don't care what people say. I have to sit around and listen to people tell me what a fool I am for jumping in the river, for getting on that trampoline. They tell me, 'You're going to have a heart attack and you're going to kill yourself. You're going to die.'

"As you know, I'm not going to die anytime soon. I'm not a fool, and I'm not an idiot, and I'm sorry they feel that way."

"One of the key scenes in the movie," remembers John, "is a picnic scene with Divine and Tab, showing them frolicking in slow motion before ants ruin their picnic. I wanted it to look like one of those deodorant commercials. Running in slow motion, every time they do it in any movie, always looks to me like a deodorant commercial. I hate that slow motion. That is the hokiest of all. So I really wanted to have the most ridiculous love montage. Also, I always loved the idea of seeing Divine in nature because it just looked ridiculous. I loved Divine, especially in *Pink Flamingos*, walking through the woods. I expected a squirrel to scream and come running out. Everything about it screamed anti-nature."

Pat Moran remembers that Glenn seemed not to notice the bigger budget and crew on *Polyester* and was always prepared, on time, and completely professional. "The love montage scene between Tab and Divy actually took quite a while to shoot. I most remember the shot where Tab and Div were making moon eyes at each other while Tab held the reigns of a beautiful black and white horse and Divine stroked the side of its head. Well, the horse wouldn't look in the right direction for the shot, and the wrangler was offscreen gesturing to get the horse to turn its head. A couple of takes into shooting, the wrangler gave the horse his cue and, instead of turning its head, it turned its body and stepped right on Divine's foot. Div was such a pro he didn't even flinch. When John yelled, "Cut!" Divine finally screamed in agony, and Tab led him over to sit down while John and the crew set up the next shot.

"Divine was really a great character actor. Just because John's movies are comical and outrageous is no reason to think that Divine was not very serious about his career."

While the film was being shot, many members of the cast and crew stayed at Pat Moran's house. Greer Yeaton, Pat Moran's daughter and Brook's sister, remembers, "Divine would come over, and he would just stay at our house. Our house was always kind of the hangout. Mink Stole lived up in the third-floor apartment during *Polyester*, and Van Smith has lived in our house before. And so my house has always been the hangout, so I've always been around Divine and everybody, really. Divine would be sleeping in the bed, and I'd come home from school, and it was like, yeah, here's Divine, he'll play Barbies with me in bed. So I'd kind of crawl up into the bed, and we'd play Barbies.

"One time I was there playing with my Barbies, and Divine fell asleep. He rolled over in the bed, and I couldn't get out. So there's some pretty funny images I have of growing up with Divine."

When *Polyester* was released, some reviewers were really turned off by the Odorama gimmick, but most of them loved Glenn and the furniture. Carrie Rickey in *Village Voice* wrote, "the color clashes and *Polyester*'s indulgent interior decoration set the scene for the Incredible Expanding Woman: Francine, wronged and abandoned by her Lothario husband, takes to the bottle and starts chewing the interiors by her very girth."

Variety saw the film as an attempt to bring John and Glenn into the mainstream. "Though trade interest centers on the participation of Tab Hunter, the pic's success depends upon a wider audience's reaction to star Divine."

Vincent Canby in *The New York Times* gave both John and Glenn their best write-up yet, calling *Polyester* "a film that demonstrates gifts for social satire that were large-ly lost in the random inspirations and insults that litter his [Waters's] earlier work. Don't panic, though. Mr. Waters still celebrates the seedy, the tacky, and the second-rate, but this time with a coherence and a wit that sharpen the point of view. Further, Divine seems to be turning into a comic actor of real style, a performer whose pres-ence in the past has always been arresting but never in particular control, but then any kind of control would have been out of place in a *Pink Flamingos* or a *Female Trouble*."

Canby singled out Glenn's perform-ance for praise: "Whether Francine Fishpaw is asking Todd Tomorrow to be gentle with her, or going on an epic booze binge as she sees the family unit disintegrate, Divine is a pricelessly funny critique of a number of high-powered Hollywood stars, includ-ing Joan Crawford, Barbara Stanwyck, and even Kim Novak in the classic *Jeanne Engels*. It also doesn't hurt that when Divine puts on one of those huge, black, massively curly wigs, he looks more than a little bit the way Elizabeth Taylor might after being locked up inside Rumpel-mayer's for three months."

I'm sure Glenn was delighted.

As Glenn and John were writ-ten up in *Variety*, *Village Voice*, and *The New York Times*, Harris and I

were going about our daily lives, still with no knowledge of where Glenn was or what he was doing.

That, of course, was soon to change.

CHAPTER 6

"John's movies are so good because there is that love
between everybody, that love and devotion to the work and to each other.
So, naturally, it comes through on the screen. Even when you're saying lines like
'I hate you' and other horrible, mean things, the love makes that better too."

—Divine, 1974 interview

Bernard Jay claims in his book that while in San Francisco during the *Neon Woman* engagement, Glenn tearfully told Bernard that he missed his parents, at which time Bernard dialed our number and handed the phone to Glenn. This is not true. And Bernard's claim that Harris's first words to Glenn were an offer to send along a pair of my earrings for him to use in his act is ridiculous. Harris never belittled Glenn in his life. As I wrote at the beginning of this book, I discovered Glenn was Divine through my friend Richard at Univis, and we got back in contact after I sent a note with Richard to Glenn at the Copa.

Of course, no matter how it happened, the important thing was that after nine long years, our baby was about to come home.

As planned, Glenn did a Halloween show at the Copa on Saturday night, and Bernard dropped him off at our house on Sunday for lunch. I made a big "WELCOME" sign for the front entrance and a cake with 36 candles and a silver star on top. I pre-

pared food that I knew he used to like to eat—roast beef, mounds of mashed potatoes and gravy, and corn on the cob. Harris and I were unbelievably excited.

When the doorbell rang and I saw him, we both started to cry. We hugged and kissed, and then Glenn saw his Dad sitting in the wheelchair and hugged and kissed him too. I remember thinking that this was all I ever wanted from Glenn, just love and respect.

After we all calmed down, I showed Glenn around the house. He loved the floor plan and said, "Mom, I know where I got my decorating abilities." He told me that the house was beautiful and he loved it.

We sat and talked while eating, and he told me about making movies for John Waters and his nightclub tours in Europe and America. He didn't say much about the early movies he'd made with John, though, and Harris and I decided not to pry. I did, however, ask him when he would take me to see his nightclub act or to a premiere of one

of his movies. He said, "Not yet, Mom. Let's wait until it's something I can really be proud of." He also asked us not to see any of the early movies, particularly *Pink Flamingos* and *Female Trouble.* (I never did have the courage to tell him that I'd already seen *Female Trouble,* and that I'd even told other moviegoers who I was and how much I enjoyed the movie.)

After three hours, Bernard Jay returned and blew the horn, and Glenn had to leave us. We hugged and kissed, and I said, "Glenn, tonight when you do your show, give it all you got. Shake it up when you sing."

He smiled and said, "I will, Mom."

Glenn introduced us to Bernard at this time, and I liked him. I thought he was a good-looking fellow with a wonderful personality. I had no inkling at all that he was the kind of person who would write and publish a mean-spirited book about Glenn and his career.

We met a lot of Glenn's friends after that. One of the first was his roommate, Jay Bennett. "I remember that initial meeting between

Div and his parents," Jay has said. "I went to his parents' house soon after to lend moral support because he was still incredibly nervous about reconciling with them. This was the first time I had met them, although Div had shown me pictures. They were really just like he had described them to me. Frances is this bigger-than-life character herself—you know, an ex-belly dancer and really gorgeous for her age. The house was grandly furnished in this amazing white and yellow Mediterranean motif. Lots of mirrors. I really loved that furniture. Harris was a quiet, very staid Southern gentleman who seemed quite content to watch his wife run around and take care of everything and entertain. There were still quite a few tears every time they greeted each other or said goodbye. They were so happy to have their son back."

Diana Evans rediscovered Glenn around this time also. "For many years, I lost track of Glenny, and someone mentioned to me that there was a drag star named Divine and that was Glenny, but I vehemently denied it. I didn't want any part of it. And then in

Father and son

1981, I saw an article about Divy living in New York, and I said, 'Yes, it is Glenn. My Glenn is Divine.' And at that point I accepted the fact that he was this performer and that was his name for the stage.

"When I discovered he was making movies for John Waters, I became upset. John was someone I had known on the periphery, but whom I never really knew that well. I think John had the inclination to lead Divine in the direction that John wanted him to go. I think that without John taking Glenn in this direction, maybe Divine would have been a wonderful stage actor or singer. He could have gone off on his own career, I think, after he really thought it through thoroughly. But he connected with a group of people who were active at the time, and he followed their lead.

"I really believe that even without John Waters, Glenn would have become a star. I think he enjoyed being fashionable, looking good, and being able to perform not as himself but as this other person."

As I have written in the early part of this book, we had struggled through our relationship during Glenn's teenage and young adult years. But during the last decade of his life, we became best friends. Sometimes, he surprised us with just how conventional he could be. One afternoon, we were looking at pictures of Harris, me, and some of our rela-

tives from the years when Glenn was not at home, and Glenn came across a picture of me standing in front of our Christmas tree in a belly-dancing costume. "What is this, Mom?"

I explained that I had taken an exercise class for women at Coral Springs High School—belly dancing for women of all ages. I enjoyed it, so after the class was over I continued to practice and even bought an

outfit from a local costume shop. Later, I was talking to the chairman of the Oakland Hills Social Club, a group that put on parties and dinners for the local retired residents, and he asked me to perform at one of the big dinner dances at a local banquet hall. The band played Greek music, and I danced my routine and put two of my veils on men in the front row. The crowd loved it, and later in the evening, a man came up to me and said he was a booking agent. He arranged shows at many of the hotels and banquet halls in southern Florida, and he offered to book me in gigs at some of the retirement condos in the area and to start a tour. I declined, but was very flattered.

As I was telling this story, Glenn got redder and redder and finally burst out, "Mom, I'm ashamed of you. Stop it right now. Please don't do anything like this again and please don't show these photographs to anyone else."

Glenn came to see us often. He talked a lot about his travels in Europe while performing, and also about his work with John Waters and the movie people in Baltimore. In between his work on *Polyester* in 1981 and *Hairspray* in 1988, released just before his death, he spent a lot of time on the road in England, Europe, New York, and Los Angeles performing his nightclub act. One of Glenn's closest friends, Anne Cersosimo, with whom I have become close, and who spent a lot of time with Glenn in Europe, has shared with me many memories from this time. I've always told her that I am a very broad-minded woman and ready to handle any stories about life on the road with Glenn and all of the parties and crazy stuff that happened. Her response has always been to laugh and say, "Fran, there's just not that much to tell." This, too, is contrary to what is written in Bernard Jay's book.

"In early 1983," Anne says, "I was living in Amsterdam, and some friends of mine were running this nightclub. It was a pretty staid yuppie-type club with ferns and brass rails catering to a straight clientele, and it really wasn't going anywhere in terms of Amsterdam nightlife, so I agreed to help the club manager pick live acts to try to liven things up. We got a list of available acts from a booking agent, and I was surprised to see Divine as the first name on the list. I didn't even know that Divine had a live act, but I thought that if a performer like Divy couldn't liven up the venue, nothing could. His engagement at the club turned out to be one his first in Europe. At this point, Divy's stage act consisted mostly of audience interaction, which usually paid off in some pretty dirty jokes at the audience members' expense, along with him singing, or rather croaking, some of his favorite songs like 'The Name Game.'

"The audience was horrified. Horrified! By the end of the performance, the audience, what little was left, sat in stunned silence. But I was fascinated by him and his act and went back the second night and used my connec-

Anne Cersosimo with Glenn at La Plume, Ibiza, September 1987

tion with the owners to visit him in his dressing room. I met him and his partner, Lee, and was surprised to find him one of the sweetest and most soft-spoken people I had ever met. It turned out that we had a mutual friend. One of his Baltimore buddies, Jack Walsh, who played a reporter in *Pink Flamingos* and used to sneak him into the saunas at Johns Hopkins University to sweat off all the makeup and hair dye after long days filming *Pink Flamingos* and *Female Trouble,* had crashed on my couch for a couple of weeks during one of his European treks. Divine and I were instantaneously best friends.

"He was received a little bit better the following night, since word of what his act was like had spread through the city. The third night, he played the gay club in town, and they were extremely annoyed with him because he had chosen to play a straight club first. In fact, after this first gig he was never welcome in the gay clubs in Amsterdam. It is important to know that the huge majority of Divy's gigs in Europe were in clubs catering to straight audiences, who loved Divine's outrageous sense of humor and admired and respected his courage. These audiences came to delight in his hilarious put-downs of audience members and his witty comebacks to hecklers as well as his surprising agility during the dance numbers, where he would do suggestive variations on early '60s dance crazes like the Dirty Boogie, the Pony, the Slide, and the Bodie Green while belting out lyrics like, 'You wimp! You wimp! Who

you callin' a blimp? I ain't your Aunt Jemima, and honey, you ain't my pimp!'

"At one rural gig in Belgium, the cabaret was owned by this straight man who lived upstairs from the club and who could only provide as the dressing room his teenage son's bedroom, which was decorated with pictures of Elvis Presley and other hilariously out-of-date Americana. At the end of the show, he brought his wife and two children in to meet Divy, who took an instant liking to both kids and played games with them at dinner.

"I became his European contact person and accompanied him to virtually all of his shows in Europe, whether in Germany, Spain, or the North countries. Typically, the day began with coffee and a very late breakfast and ended with Divy and his friends smoking marijuana, which was his only real vice, his drug of choice so to speak, unless you count food. The show could be as short as 30 minutes or as long as two hours. We would often drive for hours through the provinces on the way to the next gig, and Divy would keep everyone in stitches. Even though he didn't have lots of money or any of the visible trappings of stardom, everybody wanted to be around him and part of his inner circle.

"He did hilarious imitations of people we'd meet. Years later, when *Hairspray* was a hit, critics were talking about this amazing transformation from his monstrous and crazed roles in movies like *Female Trouble* to the loving mother to Ricki Lake. This was no surprise to me, because I'd seen all of this character in the routines he would do for us and that he would do onstage. Even his turn in 'man drag' as *Hairspray*'s racist TV station owner, Arvin Hodgepile, was a character he used to do to make fun of someone we met once while traveling to a gig in New York."

The year of our reconciliation, 1981, was the year that *Polyester* was released, John Waters' book *Shock Value* was published, and Glenn began touring to promote his second single, "Native Love." Bernard was working very hard with Glenn to launch Divine's recording and nightclub career. With all of this going on, I think it would have been extremely difficult for Glenn to continue hiding his career from us.

He traveled to clubs in New York, Chicago, San Francisco, Los Angeles, and other cities, often getting write-ups in the local press like the one that I'd seen Richard reading in the Univis cafeteria. By early 1982, Glenn had three records out: "Born To Be Cheap," "Native Love," and "Shoot Your Shot/Jungle Jezebel." He even appeared on *Good Morning America* and sang! I don't think he could have ever hidden that from us.

People sometimes ask me if I was shocked by Glenn's records, and I say, "No, I think that they are very funny and show Glenn's sense of humor." Also, Glenn had a

fondness and talent for music from a very early age, and it seemed like he was finally realizing some of his potential in a wide array of show business endeavors. Bernard and he seemed to have a strong friendship and a good business relationship.

One of the people I later met at the tribute to Glenn in London after his death was Mitch Whitehead. Mitch is Glenn's self-described "number 1 fan." The first thing Mitch did after being introduced was take off his shirt to show me a huge tattoo of Divine that covered his entire back. A smaller picture adorns his chest and simply reads "Divine."

I'll let Mitch describe his third tattoo himself. "It's a picture from *Female Trouble* on one arm with 'I'm so fucking beautiful' written underneath.

Mitch continues, "I was a roadie for Divine when he toured Britain and Europe for three years in 1985-87. I first saw him in 1983 at Rock Shots, a club in Newcastle. He came out onstage and did "Native Love" and "Love Reaction," and I just fell in love with this amazing character. It's not that I fancy women or big women, but I just thought that Divine was the greatest performer I'd ever seen.

"So I followed him around the country, slept in garages and doorways, and hitchhiked to get from club to club. Finally, Bernard had seen me around all these shows, and one day I just started helping them with the equipment. And I became part

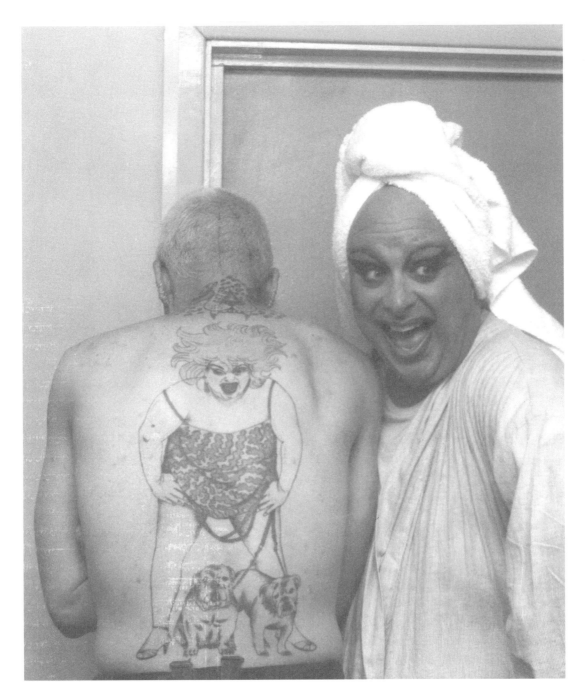

of the entourage.

"Divine was bored a lot on the road. I don't think he had much rapport or closeness with a lot of the people who traveled with him. But as soon as he walked onstage, there would be this total transformation.

"He was incredibly popular in England and Europe at this time. The Hippodrome was this huge disco in London, and Divine held the house record there for many years. Whenever he would play there, the place would be packed. The first time he played the Hippodrome, he came up out of the floor on a throne with fireworks going off all around him. All the dancers were wearing Stars-and-Stripes shorts. As he came off the throne, he pulled off their shorts one by one to reveal their Union Jack briefs underneath, and dollar bills came down from the ceiling.

"The second time, he came up from the floor wearing purple robes while sitting on the back of a baby elephant. The third time, he was supposed to come down from the ceiling on a moving platform. Everyone was expecting him to come up from the floor again. When the announcer shouted, 'Please welcome the one, the only DIVINE!' the music started, Divy started to sing, and the

Divine with Mitch Whitehead

platform wouldn't come down."

Andrew Logan has told me about Glenn's work overseas as well. "In the early to mid '80s, Divine was in London and Europe quite a lot. He would just show up and call, saying, 'What are you doing?' which meant, 'Here I am.' We would have to drop everything and look after him while he was in England. During this time he became quite an Anglophile. I would take him around in my car to show him the delights of London, but as soon as he got in the car, he would fall asleep. Also, he would always say, 'I don't want to meet any new people.' He just wanted to be with his small group of London friends. This was wonderful, but it was very hard work.

"My sister used to be his treasurer when he was on tour with his cabaret act. He used to say to her, 'No dough, no show.' He always insisted on being paid in advance.

"Once he actually appeared on the BBC's weekly TV show *Top of the Pops* to sing "So You Think You're a Man." During this time *Top of the Pops* was recorded live [as opposed to lip sync] with the performer singing to a prerecorded backing track. There was Divine, strutting his stuff onstage in front of an audience of 13- and 14-year-olds. They just sat there stunned. They couldn't believe what they were seeing."

Andrew's partner, Michael Davis, went to every show that Glenn ever did in the United Kingdom. He remembers, "I went on tour with him. At this point his act was really

unbelievable. He used to say dreadful things about dear Princess Margaret. He coughed a lot and made terrible comments about what was stuck in his throat.

"I traveled with him for a month during a German tour from one sleazy little club to another. He was a lovely person backstage. But once he started putting the makeup on, he became this absolute monster. As soon as the makeup came out of the case, I found it best to just leave him alone until after the show."

Mitch Whitehead remembers: "His comic timing was flawless. Hecklers would shout, 'Get your tits out!' and he'd fire back, 'Get your dick out!' More than once, he made the follow spot pick the guy out of the crowd. Then he'd grumble, 'Look at that. It's only Mickey Mouse meat.' They were usually pretty quiet after that.

"The worst were the student gigs in England. The crowds were mostly straight, obnoxious kids who really didn't respect him. Some of them actually thought he would like it if they threw things at him. One time in Scotland, when stuff kept flying up onto the stage, he stopped the show and walked offstage. The crowd thought it was part of the show and applauded. They were surprised when he didn't come back on."

Anne Cersosimo remembers the cabaret tours as well. "Everybody wanted to be near Divy and be part of his inner circle. Friends, fans, and acquaintances would all flock around him before and after shows and any time we would have dinner or go out for

coffee. Bernard Jay was always very jealous of me and the relationship I had with Divy. Bernard was never really there in that inner circle. He was always off doing something else. I remember Divine was always worried and would ask me, 'Can I trust him? I just don't know. I guess I can. I just don't know.'

"Much of the nightclub act was Bernard's invention. He really seemed to understand how Divy could use his image from the John Waters films and adapt that to a musical cabaret act. But as for Bernard's claims that

he was somehow Divy's caretaker, and that without him [Divy] would have gotten into 'more trouble,' that's just impossible. He wasn't there.

"Bernard was always trying to make Divy keep a journal of everything he spent money on—he was constantly buying presents for friends. In fact, I first became aware of Frances because of packages I was always mailing to Florida—Christmas balls (Divy's favorite gift for family and friends), Hummel figurines, and other accent pieces for the Milsteads' house in Florida.

"Divine wanted me to stay with him and take care of things on a day-to-day basis while he traveled, but I couldn't do this because I had children to take care of, even though I was able to travel with him quite a bit. He used to say to me, 'When you come with me, you give me credibility. When I am alone and I go into a club, people just shove me into a room and keep me there. When you come with me, people are really nice to me.' He would get really lonely. Plus, it's boring to be on the road. People think it's glamorous to travel and perform, but really it's just awful.

"When Divy would get depressed, he would overeat. He had a voracious appetite on a good day, and he loved my cooking. He told me that I made the best spaghetti sauce he had ever had, and he loved a chicken dish I made, which was a baked whole chicken with a sort of oriental sauce with tomatoes and soy sauce. Once, he ate the entire chicken at one sitting while telling stories and jokes to an astonished group of friends and onlookers.

"There were plenty of times, however, when there just wasn't that much to eat. Once we'd driven for hours to give a show in Holland for about 50 people in the middle of nowhere. The show didn't even start until 10 o'clock at night, and everyone was starving. Traveling with us at the time was Ross Sandusky, who was doing Divy's costumes and would later go on to work with Madonna. Here we were in this tiny club, and Divy is up on the stage, working the crowd and sweating profusely. I went to the bar at the back of the club and ordered something to eat. The only food for miles was this last serving of pig's feet, just a small plate of about three or four hooves with the meat on it. The club had been saving it for

Divy, and they thought I was picking it up to take it back to his dressing room. I sat at a table in the back of the club and chowed down on the last food in the place, and Divy watched me from the stage, growing more desperate and hungry as he watched me. I noticed his shoulders beginning to slump and the punch go out of his performance. But Divy never got tired of telling the story and cracking up over it.

"Since Divine's death, largely because of Bernard's book, people have heard rumors about Divy surrounding himself with young male groupies and hustlers while on tour in Europe and New York. This is the product of somebody's imagination. There were no male groupies.

"I remember how shy Divy would be when confronted by a fan who expected his behavior to be as outrageous as it was in his

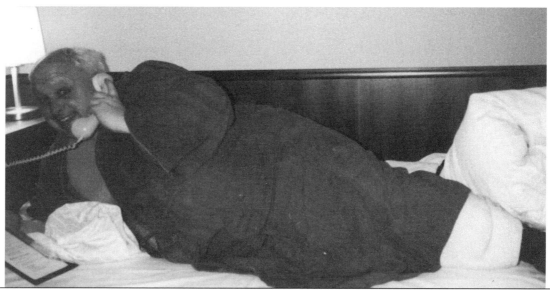

stage act or in one of John Waters's movies. After an afternoon show in Holland way out in the country, many of the fans, most of whom were straight teenagers, came backstage to meet him and get autographs. One young man pushed his way to the front of the line and, turning his back on Divy, pulled down his pants and presented his bare bottom for an autograph. Divy looked up at me like he was in shock. He simply couldn't believe it. He signed it really quickly—I had never seen his hands move that fast—and was a good sport. But as for the behavior that Bernard's book describes, I never saw Divy behave in an impolite or aggressive or promiscuous way. Ever.

"Divine often traveled with his boyfriend, Lee, who was an important part of Divy's inner circle. When Divine and Lee had a terrible falling out, Divy was despondent for weeks. And later in New York, when Lee gave me a letter to give to Divy, he was still hurting so bad he refused to open it."

"I traveled a lot with Divy in those days," Steve Friedman told me. "I went with him though England, Scotland, and Ibiza. He took a house there [in Ibiza] almost every fall. I would sometimes help him get ready for his shows, which when he was really busy could be two a night. I must say, his European act was much more on fire than his U.S. club gigs ever were. The Europeans just ate him up: It was just short of having to have bodyguards flanking the stage with linked arms keeping people from storming

the stage, unlike shows in Chicago or Dallas where we'd get to the club and there would be maybe 60 people. He would play some of the heterosexual clubs in the U.S. and get a hideous reception, abroad they were, well, European. They loved Divine.

"I'm sure that inwardly he was much more electrified by the bigger and more rabid crowds in Europe, but you'd never know that outwardly. He put on the same show for those 60 lame people in Houston as he did for 5,000 screaming fans in Europe. He was a real trooper. He put on a phenomenal show every time I saw him. When that music went on, he'd hit the stage and didn't know or care if there were 12 or 1,200 people, much less whether they were straight or gay.

"It was surrounding the records and touring that Divy had the most serious reservations about Bernard Jay on a professional level," says Steve. "Bernard wouldn't give up a gig even if it was the worst thing for Divy to be doing. In New York, Div would get booked into these hostile teenybopper clubs that were predominantly heterosexual, where at the end of the show he would have to have security guards take him out. Just a house full of 16-to-18-year-old heterosexual boys who screamed at him, mocking him and calling him those names we are all overly familiar with. But to Bernard it was a house of 3,000 or 4,000 people. So it was a great show. He saw dollars."

"Bernard Jay was very jealous of Divy's

friends, and I have to say I never liked him," says Jay Bennett. "He was my employer for a while, since he was producer of *Neon Woman*. What was good about him was that he was able to get money for Divy, but I really think that most of that work came to Divy. Bernard may have brokered the deals, but he never went out and got the work. He was not really an agent, but I have to give him credit for organizing things pretty well and doing the business part of it. But Divine should have worked more than he did and should have worked at much better things. Some of this really could have been the result of Divy's laziness. He never really was very good at promoting himself, and I think he really came to appreciate the fact that Bernard was doing some of that for him.

"Divy would always try to include Bernard in social gatherings, which could be a pretty tough fit, since Bernard wasn't really that hip. He was awkward, and he had this outlandishly cheap, cheesy style of dress, the way a bad movie would have a tacky showbiz manager dress. He didn't fit in with the hip crowd that Divy traveled with, and I think this really got to Bernard."

"I first met Divine in 1985, at the beginning of the *Lust in the Dust* project," remembers his friend, photographer Greg Gorman. "Tab Hunter had loved working with Divine on *Polyester,* and when he and Allan Glaser came up with the idea for a parody of Western movie conventions to be shot on location in the Southwest, they immediately knew that Divine would make the perfect Old West saloon girl. So with Tab and Allan trying to raise money, they brought me in to do a preliminary shoot of Divine in costume on location to help them raise some money. These photos, especially one of Div cowering and looking over her shoulder in a burlesque of the demure Western heroine, were later used to promote the film.

"I had been a huge fan of Divine's for many years, and I had been friends with Tab also. Tab loved him and was delighted to have him on board. They remained very close friends until the end of Divine's life. Tab once told *The Village Voice*'s Michael Musto, 'Divine's super. He's like Annette Funicello gone bananas in a pasta factory. Outside of his drag, he's a wonderful, kind, lovely human being.'

"I have to admit," Gorman continues, "when I met Divine, I didn't know what to expect. I was quite taken aback by just how gentle, introspective, calm, and humorous he was. Most actors, obviously, are different from the characters they play, but he was even more so. Just this incredibly wholesome character. I really expected him to be more left-of-center than he actually was.

"In addition to this shoot at the top of the project to raise money, I was also on location in New Mexico when the movie was being shot. Although I didn't shoot any production stills, I did do special photography that was used for the one-sheet, and I never failed to be impressed by Divine. From day one

through his entire career that I knew him, he was one of the most consummate pros I'd ever met."

In *Lust in the Dust*, Glenn plays Rosie Velez, a saloon girl stranded in the Southwestern town of Chili Verde. There she meets the tough owner of the local cathouse, Marguerita Ventura, played by Lainie Kazan, and a quiet gunfighter, Abel Wood, played by Tab Hunter. Everyone in town learns that there is a stash of gold nearby and the map to the treasure is tattooed on the rear ends of Rosie and Marguerita, half on each. So all the men in the cast are after the women in more ways than one. The movie is loaded with in-jokes about old Westerns, and Glenn gets a chance to shake it up as he did in his nightclub act when he sings "These Lips Were Made For Kissin', these Hips Were Made for Blissin'" to a saloon full of men.

The movie got its title from the nickname that people gave David O. Selznick's 1946 Western romance *Duel in the Sun*, which starred Jennifer Jones and Gregory Peck. Sometimes I wonder if Glenn's younger fans catch all the wonderful jokes about classic Hollywood movies in the roles that he played for John and other directors. *Lust in the Dust* is filled with jokes that refer to *Duel in the Sun*—for instance, George Masters's makeup job of dark skin and orange lipstick for Glenn, or the scenes of Rosie bathing outside and being spied on by men. When *Duel in the Sun* first opened in 1946, its outdoor bathing scenes with Jennifer Jones were controversial.

Hamming it up with Lainie Kazan, Tab Hunter, and Greg Gorman on the set of Lust in the Dust

Greg Gorman says, "On the set of *Lust in the Dust,* he was amazing. Director Paul Bartel and Tab had Divine out in the desert crawling over rocks on ledges at the Santa Fe cliffs. He knew there were rattlesnakes all over the place up there, but there was nothing he was unwilling to do. Nothing ever seemed to bother him—he was willing to try everything and gave all of his fellow actors an incredible amount of support and encouragement. On the set, Lainie Kazan kept referring to Div as 'my big sister!' I mean, you look at that movie and it's not a one-joke drag-queen-plays-saloon-girl kind of thing. Divine was a total original, almost hard to classify, a consummate actor."

Variety gave *Lust in the Dust* a good review, predicting it would do well, and recognized it as a vehicle for Glenn's talent. "The picture is Divine's for the taking, and take it he does with a vibrant, inventive comic performance. Divine's naughty, suggestive reactions are often riotous, and his eyes prove constantly alive and expressive on camera. Co-producer Hunter need do little but imitate Clint Eastwood's muffled Man With No Name line readings, and he does this efficiently, while Kazan matches Divine wisecrack for wisecrack and, in the inevitable barroom catfight, punch for punch, in a deliciously salacious turn." *Time* magazine called the final piecing together of the puzzle on Rosie and Marguerita's bottoms "the year's most resistible shot."

The following year, 1985, Glenn was

cast in what many consider his best role outside of a John Waters movie, as gangster Hilly Blue in Alan Rudolph's *Trouble in Mind.* The movie is about a corrupt ex-cop named Hawk, played by Kris Kristofferson, who is released from prison and tries to redeem himself by protecting the innocent Georgia, played by Lori Singer, while her husband Coop, played by Keith Carradine, descends into a life of crime. *Trouble in Mind* looks and feels like those old Humphrey Bogart crime movies of the '40s in which everybody is dressed in trench coats and steps out of the shadows smoking a cigarette.

Glenn's character, Hilly Blue, a gay crime boss, is talked about for the first half of the film, and his power is hinted at by the threats of his henchman, Rambo, played by Dirk Blocker. Glenn makes his entrance in a dark Chinese restaurant as violins play Pachelbel's Canon in D on the soundtrack. It's a great entrance, and he is both quiet and threatening in this scene with Carradine and Joe Morton. Hilly's speech about his lust for money and power sounds like a crazy version of Glenn's own desire for wealth and stardom. "Most people imagine me to be a very patient person, whereas I'm just the opposite. The very moment I want something, I have to have it. Nothing ever satisfies

Director Paul Bartel and Divine between takes

123

me. Everything comes too late. Too late for me, and I get eaten up inside. When is it going to happen? When?"

Hilly Blue gets his just desserts in the end, shot between the eyes by Hawk. Glenn told his friends he loved the squibs (exploding blood packs) they used for gunshot wounds. While promoting the film, Alan Rudolph had high praise for Glenn's abilities: "I'm really happy with the way he worked out. There are some scenes in which he is really marvelous. He plays a gangster, and I don't know anything about gangsters, except that they are lethal fools, so that's how I presented them. It's a personal view, not perhaps a very serious one. It's just how I see them."

Critics either loved the movie's '40s-style look, or they saw it as a bad joke. *Variety* said, "Sometimes it's intriguing and sometimes it falls flat." *Variety* also noted, "Kingpin of the underworld Hilly Blue [is] played by Divine in his first male role after winning recognition in drag in a series of John Waters pictures…. It's hard to know what to make of Divine in man's clothes, but it is that kind of hit-or-miss mystery on which *Trouble in Mind* is built." Of course, Hilly Blue wasn't Glenn's first male role, even though it was he is first *big* male role.

Among the reviewers who praised Glenn were Brian Baxter, who wrote in the English magazine *Films and Filming*, "In a supporting role, a richly discordant note is struck by a brassy instrument—Divine," and David Denby, who commended Alan Rudolph for "ha[ving] the wonderful idea of putting the female impersonator Divine in a suit for a change and setting him up as a silky Sydney Greenstreet crime lord."

Some reviewers, though, just couldn't get past their image of Glenn in John Waters's movies. Pauline Kael in *The New Yorker* called Hilly Blue a "semi-male role," and said Glenn was "made up to look like a plump plucked chicken." Walter Goodman in *The New York Times* said Divine "gives camp a bad name as a gang leader who hates his mother."

Around the time that *Trouble in Mind* hit the theaters, Glenn invited us to visit him at his place in Key West. We went there with his little Yorkies that he had left with us up north. Jay prepared the meal, and Glenn showed us around the house. Everything was neat and not at all like the disaster his bedroom had been while growing up in Baltimore.

After dinner, Glenn decided to show me around Key West and go shopping. He needed a toaster and air conditioner. Jay went with us. We went to Sears, and Glenn picked out the most expensive air conditioner and asked me if I would charge it and he would pay me back. We walked around the mall having a good time. Glenn was always pointing out things that he thought were

124

interesting, either because they caught his eye or because he found them ridiculous. The mall was a great place for this. Then we went home, had a snack, and went to bed.

"Yes, I remember the shopping trip to Sears," says Jay. "These were the kind of shenanigans we were famous for. Div and I both loved to shop, and I have to admit I actually have known people who ended up in a 12-step group for compulsive shopping. I don't think that Glenn was 12-step powerless over his shopping, but he was definitely good at wangling ways to live beyond his means. It was never out-and-out stealing, but people were always 'lending' him things or money. Nothing was purposeful, but we would get into a jam where we couldn't pay people back, and I think the thing with Frances at Sears was one of those times. I know he never paid her back."

Sometimes Bernard would come with Glenn to visit us. According to Bernard, Glenn's bills were all paid, including his income taxes. It seemed like there was nothing to worry about with Glenn anymore, even though he never paid me back for the air conditioner. Bernard and I got along beautifully, and I took to calling him my "number 2 son," and he called me his "number 2 Mom." We enjoyed each other's company; we exchanged gifts and would see each other when he came to Florida to visit his relatives who lived nearby.

Others who got along with Bernard were just as shocked as I was when Bernard's

book was published and portrayed Glenn in such a negative light.

"I got along great with Bernard Jay," says photographer Greg Gorman. "And he had nice things to say about me in the biography he wrote on Divine. But I felt that there was so much hostility and so much mean-spiritedness in the way Divine was portrayed in the book that was just 180 degrees from who he was. I couldn't say one negative thing about [Divine], because in all those years I never had one experience that wasn't a memorable, favorable, fond experience of the man.

"I've been on a million trips with Divine to London and Europe, and I've stayed up at his place in Stoneridge in upstate New York. And I always had a great time with him. He was one of my all-time favorite friends, and his passing was one of the great losses of my life. He was one of the funniest and most quick-witted people I have ever met. We were at a club concert in L.A. once where Divine was performing, and all of a sudden, the whole crowd just swayed from one end of the club to another, and it turned out that someone had stabbed a police officer. So Divine is up there onstage sweating and going nuts, and his immediate response is, 'Well, you see it took a murder to upstage me!'

"He would constantly be doing a spoof of the Divine character around all of his friends. We were having dinner together at the Muse restaurant in Provincetown once, and everybody will tell you how much Divy

Steve Friedman and Glenn

loved to eat. We were ordering, and Div had this incredibly soft voice, almost a whisper. The waiter had to bend down almost to the center of the table to hear him murmur, 'I'll have a Caesar salad and the pork chops with the fettuccini on the side.' Suddenly, the dining room shook with the booming, inimitable Divine voice: 'AND DON'T BRING ME ANY OF THOSE FAG PORTIONS!'

"I think that Divine spent more time with his own personal friends than he did with Bernard, and I think that got to Bernard a little bit. I don't think he was as much on the inside of Divine's life as he wanted to be. I don't want to say anything bad about Bernard Jay as a person, but I thought the book portrayed Divine in a much more negative light than was proper, because he just wasn't that sort of person."

On Glenn's 40th birthday we had a party. He invited Steve Friedman, Jay Bennett, Bernard Jay, and Sharon and Frank Kujan, close friends who lived in Boca Raton, for dinner. We had a cake and ice cream, and we all had a great time. It was like the old days in more than one way. After dinner, Glenn and our five guests quickly excused themselves from the table, assuring Harris and me that they would be right back. About 15 minutes later they came back, and our conversation continued. I immediately noticed that they were acting even sillier

Glenn with close friend Greg Gorman in Ibiza, 1987

than usual, and it didn't take me long to realize that they had sneaked back to the bedroom, shoved pillows under the door, and smoked marijuana. At least they didn't beat it out the back door as Glenn's high school friends had done years before!

When I prepared dinner, Steve Friedman always helped me in the kitchen. Even though Glenn was a wonderful cook, when he came home, he wanted Mom to take care of the cooking. All that he ever contributed were bottles and bottles of Mouton Cadet red wine. Harris and I didn't drink, but Glenn and his friends usually took up the slack. Steve, on the other hand, always helped with cutting up vegetables, rinsing out saucepans, and doing the dishes at the end of the evening. I used to say, "Steve, you are a bitch in the kitchen!" We laughed a lot and enjoyed each other. That was his nickname: "Bitch in the Kitchen."

One day I met Glenn at the airport, and I started to laugh when I saw him. He had on a T-shirt hanging down to his knees with the word "SMILE" in big black letters on the front. It looked like hell. I asked if he couldn't wear anything that looked good on him. He smiled and said it was comfortable. He spent so much of his time in the public eye being Divine that I think he really enjoyed relaxing with his family and friends wearing whatever he wanted and just being Glenn. In fact, when we were together, he was virtually never recognized. I guess people were always expecting this larger-than-life creature with teased hair and six-inch eyebrows.

Still, he never really did grow up. Greg Gorman says, "I went to see him in Ibiza the last year, in the fall of 1987. He always took a house there in the fall. I'd flown in from London, and Divine had said, 'I'll pick you up.'

"So I get to the airport—classic, no Divine. I had no fucking idea where I was going, and there was no phone at the house where he was staying. I had no idea what to do, so I got in the car and found my way to the center of town and parked the car, figuring he'd have to surface somewhere. And, sure enough, there he came, in one of those 'SMILE' T-shirts he always wore, walking through the center of town.

"We got back to the house, and he informed me, 'I'm having a big dinner party for you tonight. I've got about 25 kids coming by for dinner.'

"'That's great. What's going on?'

"'Well, I thought we'd maybe have some chicken.'

"Guess who had to cook the chicken? I had to go out there with no wood, no nothing. I had to pull up a bunch of dead wood around the yard and some from a field nearby, build a fire, and cook 25 chickens. He entertained while I cooked. God, I miss him."

Glenn was unreliable sometimes. I remember that at Halloween of that same year, 1987, Glenn was doing a show in Miami. The next day he called and told me he was calling a cab to bring him home to have dinner with us. We expected him

Glenn did what he wanted to do no matter what people said, and performer. That, I think, is what it truly means to "walk like a man."

around 1 o'clock in the afternoon. I had a roast beef dinner cooked and had made homemade bread, which was his weakness. I didn't help his weight problem much. I just wanted to see him happy, and I knew he liked to eat. So all of the food was set out for a late lunch. And Harris and I waited for him to show up.

About 4 o'clock we heard hollering outside. I ran out to see what was going on. Glenn and the cab driver were in a shouting match. "Don't you know how to drive? Can't you follow directions? Are you a moron?" Glenn screamed. His face was beet red, and sweat poured off of his forehead.

"You take the ride, you pay the fare!" hissed the driver.

Glenn glared down at the man and began to scream even louder, for once in real life looking like one of his crazy characters in John's movies.

"What's this all about?" I asked.

Glenn said, "I told the dumb driver how to come here, and he wouldn't listen, and now he wants to charge me $40 for a $30 fare."

This could go on all night, I thought. So I asked for the driver's name and went inside to call the cab company. It took me a while, but I finally got through to the supervisor. While all of this was going on, Glenn stood on the sidewalk outside the house, pouting like a 10-year-old. I came out of the house and told the driver that his manager wanted to speak to him. He looked at me and then at Glenn, and I thought, *If looks could kill,*

Glenn and I would be dead as mackerels on the pavement right now.

A few minutes later the driver emerged from the house, and he charged Glenn the lower fare. Glenn was satisfied, and he walked into the house to see Harris. He didn't speak to me or thank me. As I followed him inside, I got the uncomfortable feeling that we were back at the old house and Glenn was still unable to fight his battles without my help. I thought later that evening, *After 40 years, why do I still feel I have to do his dirty work? He could have made that call himself.*

He had brought me a floral arrangement, which we set out on the table next to the now-cold dinner. It was made with silk flowers and was one of the most beautiful arrangements I had ever seen. I kept it for a long time.

Glenn also brought some of his interviews and press clippings. It seemed that every time we saw him, he would bring a new box of things for us to keep. The wall of secrecy between us and his other life had come crashing down, and he delighted in sharing his success with us. I have kept everything he ever brought us, and I treasure it all.

One of the nicest things he ever did was to dedicate one of his disco singles, "Walk Like a Man," to his dad and me. Every time I hear the record, I think of the scorn he endured in junior high and high school, being told he walked like a girl. Of course,

e found a way to touch many lives through his talents as a

Glenn did what he wanted to do no matter what people said, and he found a way to touch many lives through his talents as a performer. That, I think, is what it truly means to "walk like a man."

Glenn always told us that he never liked to watch himself onscreen. Over the years, so many people have told me that it took them a long time to reconcile the loud, energetic, public Divine with the shy and soft-spoken Glenn. I think there were times that he felt the same way. Also, he burned to do a role that would take him beyond the cult of the outrageous Divine and into the world of mainstream show business where his true talent as an actor could be appreciated by fans and professional peers. He wanted to do work that he could show to Harris and me with pride. I can't emphasize enough how important this was to Glenn in the last years of his life.

Belle Zwerdling of Progressive Artists talent agency in Los Angeles booked Glenn's movie and TV appearances from 1985 until his death. "I got a call from Neal Konigsberg at the publicity firm PMK," Belle says. "And he asked, 'What do you think of Divine?' I said, 'My God, I'm a huge fan of his. I'm from Baltimore.' 'Well,' Neal said, 'he's looking for representation.' That was the beginning of a wonderful friendship. Divy and I had a meeting and fell in love. I remember the first time he and Bernard Jay came to my office. When Div came into my office, as he did every time I ever saw him, he just radiated gentleness. He was nothing like the public Divine. After just a few minutes of talking with him, I was entranced.

"Bernard was an extremely organized person who was clearly in charge of the business side of Divy's career. His area of specialization was the booking of club dates and recording deals, and I was to handle the booking of Div's movie and TV work. I came to see that Bernard and Divy had an incredibly complex relationship. It was clear that Div was very dependent on Bernard, not just financially but emotionally as well.

"As I got to know Div better, I came to realize that he desperately wanted out of the never-ending cycle of touring and performing the Divine character. But it paid a lot of money, and Divy was constantly in debt.

"Someone told me that it had been suggested that Div had an addiction to shopping and was a compulsive spender. 'Suggested?' I said incredulously. He was killing a lot of pain, there's no question about it. He was heavy, and he was in a town of beauty. It was hard. And to kill the pain he went out and he shopped. And he ate. And he smoked a lot of pot. He came into my office one day, and while I was finishing up some business on the phone. He was sitting in the waiting area, and suddenly I heard a deafening crack and a thump. I put down the receiver and heard his voice, almost a

whisper from the other side of the door. "Belle? Oh, Belle? You didn't really need that couch, did you, dear?" I came running out to see what had happened, and he had flattened the sofa. We made a big joke about it, but that had to be devastating. And he was always facing the weight issue every moment that he was alive.

"He wasn't in Los Angeles a lot, but we became very close friends. He was like an old girlfriend, and when we went out to dinner we gossiped like two hags and ate until we closed out the restaurant. He just touched something deeply in me.

"Professionally, it could be a challenge to place him. He came with a lot of bag-gage. But I will say this, when it came down to performing his craft as an actor, he was beyond professional. He wasn't on time, he was early. He always knew his lines, and he never complained and never was difficult."

I'm not surprised that Belle remembers her dinners with Glenn. He definitely had a passion for food. One weekend when he came home, I had baked his favorite cake, and Daniel Wenger, a friend of his from Boca Raton who was usually an exercise-and-health nut, was there. I had taken the cake out of the oven to let it cool before icing it. But that never happened. Glenn and Daniel ate the whole cake while it was warm. Sometimes when Steve Friedman

Zandra Rhodes, Glenn, Chuck Yeaton, and Pat Moran shopping for munchies in Baltimore

came home with him, I could hear them raid-ing the refrigerator in the middle of the night. Maybe this had something to do with all of those pillows shoved under the door in Glenn's room!

When in Miami, Glenn would rent a room at one of the hotels close to the club where he was playing. That's where he would keep all of his costumes, makeup, and props. He would get ready for the show at the hotel. Steve would usually help him get into costume and makeup, and then the two of them would take a hired car to the club. After the show they would go back to the hotel. Glenn would get out of costume, and they would go out with friends or have peo-ple come visit them at the hotel.

Whenever Glenn came to see Harris and me, he would have on no trace of his costume or makeup except for those shaved eyebrows, which I must admit were sometimes distract-ing. He never brought along his costumes when he visited, either. I am always amazed when people ask me if Glenn ever came to dinner dressed in six-inch heels and a fright wig. "My son was an actor," I tell them.

Near the end of 1987, Glenn told his dad and me that as a gift for our 50th wed-ding anniversary he was planning to put in a pool. Harris was against the idea. But Glenn threatened to stop coming home and walked back into his bedroom. It meant a lot to him to be able to pay Harris and me back in some way for all of the years that we had supported him. Now that he was doing well

in his career, it hurt him that we would reject his offer.

After Glenn cooled off, he came back to the living room to talk again. He said it would be nice to come home and be able to swim in a backyard pool rather than to go to the beach, and that we could entertain friends at poolside. He was going to design the pool and put in a wheelchair lift so Harris could exercise. He made it sound so enticing that Harris and I gave in.

Glenn and I talked to several pool builders, and we decided to build the pool with a screened enclosure. Glenn also went to a nursery and let them know what he wanted planted around the outside of the screen. Then he ordered a six-foot privacy fence. This was all to be completed by Easter of 1988 at a cost of $20,000. "You'll be happy with it when it's done," Glenn said.

We decided to have a giant pool party at Easter. But, unfortunately, the party was to never to be.

CHAPTER 7

"All of Baltimore knows I'm big, blond, and beautiful."

—Tracy Turnblad (Ricki Lake), *Hairspray* (1988)

Earlier in 1987, Glenn and John Waters had finished shooting *Hairspray,* the movie that would make my Glenn a real star beyond underground films, fringe comedies, and nightclubs. *Hairspray* was a PG-rated musical comedy that looked back on the early '60s in Baltimore—all the crazy music and fashions. It wasn't just nostalgia, though. The plot centers on Tracy Turnblad, an overweight but energetic teenage girl (played by Ricki Lake) who becomes the most popular dancer on a local TV dance show. She and her "upper lower-class" parents, Wilbur and Edna (played by Jerry Stiller and Glenn), come to support the integration of the dance show, while Tracy's rival for Miss Auto Show 1962, the snobbish Amber Von Tussle (played by Colleen Fitzpatrick), lobbies against desegregation.

Here at last was a movie and a role that Glenn was proud to share with Harris and me. In *Hairspray* he got a chance to show a little bit of the real Glenn behind Divine in his role as Edna, a loving mom to Ricki Lake's Tracy. He also showed us a character who has a change of heart and learns to embrace people different from herself. "It's the times,

Harold," she says to her husband. "They are a' changin'. Somethin's blowin' in the wind. Fetch me my diet pills, wouldja hon?"

"*Hairspray* was crucial for the plans Divine and I had for his career," confides Belle Zwerdling. "We had worked so hard to move Div away from the raunchy Divine character and to get him roles in male dress. It was so important to Glenn to be seen as something other than the fat monster from movies like *Pink Flamingos* and *Female Trouble.* Glenn loved John, but he wanted desperately to be seen as a star in his own right, not just part of this Baltimore repertory company.

"One of the great things that John did on the film, which we asked for and he did brilliantly, was to include a small male role for Div so the movie wouldn't usurp everything we'd been doing. Arvin Hodgepile, the racist TV station owner, was so convincing a bigoted loudmouth that many fans didn't even recognize their favorite star until the end credits, where the actor playing Arvin is shown to be Divine."

Hairspray's TV dance program, *The Corny Collins Show,* was actually based on

134

"Every one of my movies is about someone who takes what socie people take more abuse than any other minority."

The Buddy Deane Show that Glenn, John, and all of their friends used to run home and watch after school every day when they were young. John told *The New York Times,* "*Hairspray* was based on my memory and my exaggeration of a show that was a big influence on me. There really was a dance called the Roach, where you squash something and spray your partner, and the Bug, where you jump into a circle and scratch and then throw 'it' to another person and they scratch. I actually did all those old dances for startled executives at 10 A.M. in their office to make a pitch for the film."

That wasn't the only realistic element in the film. "Baltimore at the time was incredibly racially tense," John told Steve Yeager years later. "It was when everything was becoming integrated. With *The Buddy Deane Show,* it really did happen. They didn't know what to do about it, because it was all black music with white kids dancing to it. And the white kids on the show would have let blacks come on and dance. It was their parents who wouldn't allow that kind of integration, which was unheard of at the time. They said the same things that Divine said as Arvin Hodgepile, 'Baltimore is not ready for integrated dancing.' I just gave it a happier ending than in real life."

Buddy Deane, now retired and living in Arkansas, spoke of the less happy real-life ending to the racial tension surrounding his old show. "When all this started to happen and the pickets came outside of WJZ, the

station that carried my show, I knew we were in trouble, the show was ending. It was at the end of its run, and the TV station just couldn't handle it. The management called me in and said, 'Well, we can't integrate the show, so that's it.'"

Belle Zwerdling recently told me, "When shooting started on *Hairspray,* Divy called me up to say hello, and I said, 'Are you excited?'

"He said, 'Oh, I'm really excited. This is wonderful.'

"'Tell me what your trailer's like.'

"There was a little pause on the other end of the line. He said, 'Well, I don't really have a trailer.'

"'What do you mean?' I asked somewhat sternly.

"'Well, I'm in the makeup room, and I have a wooden couch to lie down on. You know.'

"'No, I don't know. What do you think? How about the other cast members?'

"'Well, Pia Zadora has a trailer, and Sonny Bono has a trailer—'

"I cut him off. 'Do you mind if I cause a bit of a stir?'

"'No, go ahead,' he replied.

"As soon as I rang off with Divy, I called Stanley Buchthal, the producer, and told him that I was pulling Divine off the film if he didn't get a trailer the size of Pia's or Sonny's. The next day he had it. Div never let on to anyone on the set that this was an issue. He was a model of professionalism and generosity."

says is a disadvantage and turns it into a style and wins. And fat

"Divine and Ricki Lake struck up a wonderful friendship on the set of *Hairspray*," remembers John Waters. "They were both big, blond, and beautiful. I think the only thing that Ricki had trouble with was when we really bleached her hair out that color, which was bright yellow. She almost had a nervous breakdown.

"People wondered if Divine was jealous, because Divine wanted to play that role, certainly, before we started, and in the old days he would have. Don't forget: In *Female Trouble* he played a teenager when he was near 30. But he realized, I think, that the better the actress, the better he looked too. So he knew Ricki was good, and I think they did bond very well. They really did become like mother and daughter during the making of the movie."

Glenn had a great sense of humor about working opposite Ricki. He told *Interview* magazine, "I wanted to do it, to play mother and daughter, like those Lana Turner movies where she's 16 years old and then she's 80. I thought it would add the right touch. But I think the producers were a bit leery, so they hired Ricki Lake to be my daughter. She's 19 and delightful. I hate her. I've got to admit, some of those kids were a little young, and no matter what kind of makeup I devised, I wouldn't have held up next to a real 15-year-old boyfriend. The camera is so unkind."

Ricki had a sense of humor about all of this too. When the film came out, she was featured in an interview piece in *The Village Voice* written by Barry Walters. "Lake is just like Tracy—totally adorable. She's the perky flip side of all those foulmouthed delinquents Divine played in the old days, but with the same amount of spunk. Although she's making her screen debut in the greatest John Waters film yet, Ricki is still a lady: 'I was worried that because I played Divine's daughter people would think I was a man, especially because my name is Ricki,' she recalls, as she rips open her blazer, 'but not with these tits!'"

John pointed out to *The New York Times* that Tracy is a lot like the heroines of his earlier, more shocking movies: "Every one of my movies is about someone who takes what society says is a disadvantage and turns it into a style and wins. And fat people take more abuse than any other minority."

Ricki is a very sweet person, and she has been so nice to me since Glenn's death. She has nothing but praise for him as an actor. "Working with Divine was fantastic," she says. "He was a consummate professional. I remember it was the summer of 1987. There were cicadas everywhere. It was Baltimore in the summertime. It was 100 degrees with 100 percent humidity—just nasty. And we were shooting in these little tiny stores and little tiny sets, and he would sweat because he had the wig on and the makeup covering his beard, and he never complained. I never once heard him complain. He always had the best attitude, and I think I learned so much

about how to be a professional and how to work in this business by watching him and watching John.

"And he was really good to me. I remember he was the one who taught me how to walk in high heels because I had never, you know, I had *never* worn anything but Keds sneakers before. And so he really took me by the hand and said, 'No, no, you've got to do it like this,' and made me copy him."

For the dance scenes, John and Pat Moran hired expert choreographer Ed Love, who had danced on Broadway and choreographed music videos for Tina Turner, Natalie Cole, and Whitney Houston. Love told *Dance* magazine how carefully the dances were choreographed. "I am happy that the way the white kids' dance scenes were shot contrasts sharply with what you see when the camera moves into the black neighborhoods," he said. "The dancers on *The Corny Collins Show* are white, and even though they do dances such as the Roach, which has black origins, there's no soul to it, really. But the black dancers from the fringe neighborhoods doing the Slow Drag and the Dirty Boogie really let loose. They didn't have to worry about looking pristine or avoiding the TV censors, since they weren't allowed to be on the show anyway.

"It's horrible that Divine, who was symbolic of the John Waters aesthetic, died on the verge of his greatest success. He became a reference for all of us who needed to know what John stood for. He would be thrilled that *Hairspray* has become a mainstream hit. We all knew it was going to be risky doing something for a wide audience, but John managed to retain his own bad taste and integrity. It feels good to be a part of it."

John's cameraman David Insley describes work on the set of *Hairspray*: "We talked about what *The Buddy Deane Show* looked like and what dance TV shows looked like at the time, and we ended up lighting all the dance studio stuff as if it was a TV set. We ended up getting old lighting fixtures that they used in the '50s and '60s in TV studios, and we used them as our lighting sources. So we had all these scoops up in the ceiling of the studio, you know, which are just essentially big, soft floodlights. We said, 'We'll have three cameras on the dances, and one of them will be on the ground and two of them will be up in the air.' We would usually run three cameras, and after we got it once from those three positions, we'd change around and do it from another three positions. They would go through the whole dance, and we'd cover it."

Ricki remembers, "It was hot as hell under all of those old TV lights. Every time that I wasn't on screen, I was on the side practicing the Mashed Potato and stuff. I think I lost like 20 pounds like that, because I wasn't used to exercising. And they would feed me DoveBars, you know. They were called fat patrols. Divine would chase me around with a DoveBar to try to help me put on weight so the continuity would match.

Glenn and godson Brook Yeaton on the final day of Hairspray *shoot*

Plus, he knew all of the dances in that movie from his high school days—every one. He would show them to me and Michael St. Gerard. Divine was amazing."

"When Divine played Edna," remembers John, "the very first day I saw him dressed like that and he walked on the set, I didn't recognize him. I thought he was one of the ladies in the neighborhood. He played it completely realistically. I think the natural and believable dimension of Divine's role in *Hairspray* was why it worked. But underneath it all you knew that this very normal mother was played by a man, which, let's face it, doesn't very often happen.

"I remember Divine dressed like that, in a housecoat and greasy wig held back with hairpins, trudging across the studio floor in house slippers and saying, 'No one can ever call me a drag queen again. What drag queen would allow herself to look like this? I look like half the women from Baltimore.' And he's right. That's acting; that ain't drag."

Glenn had always enjoyed working with John. Although they had been close friends for years, it could get tense on the set of *Hairspray* as on all the earlier movies, "When John is working on a movie," Glenn said, "he's still your friend, but it's a director-actor relationship. That's what makes it difficult for a lot of people involved, because we are all close friends and have been for many, many years. So it's very hard to keep the personal out of the whole thing. When something is said from the director, who is John, it's very hard not to take that personally. Sometimes people do, and that creates some of the bad moments, the hazards of working with a friend. But that's not very often. He gets very nervous, I think, when he's working on a film, because he's captain of the ship or whatever, so he feels he has to hold it all together. I mean, a lot of us can be so childlike at times—I know that I can. We are all under a lot of pressure, but he has to worry about all of us, plus the film, plus the financial part of it, plus the distributors—all of that. So he is completely different when he is the director. When he's not, he's much more tender and loving—not that he's not when we're work-

Glenn and Mink Stole at premiere of Hairspray

138

ing. Still, everyone is more or less very, very cooperative with John. We all feel he's extremely talented. He's done a lot for all of us as far as careers go in show business or the entertainment field. None of us were involved in the business at all before John started making the films."

Mink Stole, who has been with John and Glenn from the earliest days, has fond memories of filming *Hairspray*. "There was just one moment where Divine and Chris Mason, who was doing our hair, and I just—I don't remember what it was, but we just wanted out, just for a minute. We were filming at the Palladium, a big auditorium-banquet hall in Baltimore we were using for the auto show set. It was the day of the car show, and there were all these beautiful Lincoln convertibles. Divine and Chris and I just ran out and grabbed one with a driver, and I think we probably went for a half-mile drive in full makeup, all our wigs on, no scarves. And it was so childish and so innocent. We were just being grown-up brats just for a minute. And I really loved it. It was just really, really fun. Because we were good kids. I mean, if John was our father, then we had all been very, very good children, and this was just our one breakout moment."

Brooke Yeaton, Glenn's godson and the movie's prop master, remembers that "the day they wrapped on *Hairspray*, Divine closed his dressing room door and wouldn't let anyone in at all. But then I got the call over the walkie-talkie to come in, and he was weep-

ing, just sitting in his chair in front of the mirror crying. I think he knew it would be the last time that he would be working with John, and I think that he knew it was the only time he and I would be working together. It was an incredibly emotional moment."

Christmas, 1987 was just beautiful. I had the tree and the house all decorated, but it wasn't enough to please Glenn, so we had to go shopping for more lights, decorations, and gifts for everyone who was invited.

Glenn's Aunt Doris came to visit, and we decided to go to a U-Pick'em farm. We asked Glenn to go with us for the ride. He slept most of the way. When we arrived at the farm, I gave Doris and him each a bucket.

"What is this bucket for?" asked Glenn.

"To help pick fresh vegetables," I said. "You can pick strawberries."

"You and Aunt Doris can go pick your stuff, and I'll stay here and pick my nose."

There were a few people standing nearby who overheard the conversation, and they laughed because it sounded so funny. The whole episode made me think of how far we had come as a family since the early days back in Grindstone, Pennsylvania, where we kids had to work the farm for the family to survive.

We were tired when we got home, and Glenn sat down on the sofa to talk to his dad but fell asleep, as often happened. Glenn's tendency to doze off had begun to worry me. He also had shortness of breath, and I worried about that too. "Glenn," I said, "You need to go to a doctor to try to lose weight." He promised that he would when he went to New York after Christmas.

New Line Cinema had done a lot of pre-release publicity for *Hairspray,* and the news media had gotten wind that Glenn had come home for Christmas. The press wanted to come and take photos of our tree and dinner table, but I refused.

Glenn was thrilled about *Hairspray's* imminent release. He said, "Mom, when they have the world premiere in February in Baltimore, I want to take you with me." Well, that really hit me because it was the first time Glenn had invited me to go with him. Tears came to my eyes, I was so happy. Glenn said, "I told you that when I did a movie I was proud of and thought you would enjoy, I would ask you. So here is your chance. Go and buy a pretty dress to wear." Since Harris could not go to the premiere, Glenn had brought him a special videocassette of *Hairspray* as a Christmas gift.

Glenn had to leave for New York the day after Christmas. He had just rented a penthouse near Central Park and had a lot of work to do before going to England to do a New Year's show. I knew he was tired and just wanted to rest. But he never complained. Bernard had given him a pocket-size TV that he could watch while on the plane. Glenn often fell asleep in first class and would start

snoring, which would aggravate the other passengers. They'd complain to the flight attendant, who would come by and tap Glenn on the arm. Usually, Glenn woke up easily with a smile on his face—only to fall asleep and start snoring again. Bernard hoped the TV would help him stay awake.

Glenn called us while he was in London, and we talked about the wonderful Christmas we'd had, and we continued planning for Easter. Everyone who had come for Christmas had seen the pool, though not completed, and they had all been invited to come back for Easter Sunday. And of course, everyone had accepted the invitation.

January and February saw many press

140

screenings of *Hairspray,* timed so the reviews would appear as the movie was being released. For those of us stunned by the loss of Glenn and the publicity his death generated for the movie in its first weeks of release, it is important to remember that almost all of the wonderful notices for *Hairspray* and Glenn's performance were written in the final few weeks *before* his death.

The reviews for the movie were raves. *Rolling Stone* called it "a family movie both the Bradys and the Mansons could adore: affectionate, liberal, and deeply subversive, with a 400-pound transvestite who balloons out of his housedresses, a fat girl who outshimmies the skinnies, and a lanky black boy who smooches his blond, baby-faced girlfriend and sighs, 'My little white lily,' while the reflection of the ghetto moon ripples in the rat-infested gutter." *New York* magazine said, "This movie, which truly feels as if it had been made inside a hairspray can, has great heart." Pauline Kael wrote in *The New Yorker* wrote, "John Waters treats the

message movie as a genre to be parodied, just like the teenpic. Combining the two, he comes up with an entertainingly imbecilic musical comedy—a piece of pop Dadaism."

Every part of the movie was singled out for praise: the acting, sets, costumes, hair, and dances. Janet Maslin in *The New York Times* said, "The director of *Pink Flamingos* and *Female Trouble* has no need to deliberately offend, since the characters and costumes of *Hairspray* so handily do the job for him. There's no shade of mustard or chartreuse too awful to be recreated here, no figure of teenage speech too stupid, no fad too trendy." *Variety* said, "Special credit should go to hair designer Christine Mason, who made every woman in the cast look as though she's wearing frozen cotton candy on her head, and costume designer Van Smith, whose period re-creations provoke constant amusement."

But it was Glenn's performance as both Edna Turnblad and Arvin Hodgepile that was most constantly singled out for praise. *Variety* said, "Divine, so big he wears a tent-like garment big enough for three ordinary mortals to sleep in, is in otherwise fine form in a dual role." David Denby of *New York* magazine wrote, "At home, in a custom-paneled TV room, Divine (the female impersonator and Waters' superstar) stands in a sleeveless print dress ironing, endlessly ironing. Divine reigns in dyspeptic dismay over Waters' eternal lower-middle-class Baltimore, a movie landscape by now as familiar as John Ford's Monument Valley." *The Times* noted, "The actors are best when they avoid exaggeration and remain weirdly sincere. That way, they do nothing to break the vibrant, even hallucinogenic spell of Mr. Waters' nostalgia. As Tracy's mother, Divine barges through the film in a housedress and pin curls, looking something like a wildly dressed refrigerator but sounding a lot more amusing. Divine also has another, smaller role, this time as the bigoted man who runs the television station that airs Corny's show. (In a man's suit, Divine manages to look only half-dressed.)" *The Times* called Edna "a great, cheerful, eye-boggling cartoon. Even when her diet pills are wearing off, she's forever patient with her difficult daughter. She's the voice of reason in adversity ('Remember, you can't change the world's problems in one day'), though occasionally she does get exasperated ('Once again, your hairdo has

gotten you in hot water'). When the chips are down, though, she enthusiastically supports Tracy's leap toward stardom." Pauline Kael summed it up when she wrote, "It's really Divine's movie; he watches over Tracy and preens like a mother hen. There's a what-the-hell quality to his acting and his funhouse-mirror figure which the film needs; it would be too close to a real teenpic without it. When Divine's Edna Turnblad is onscreen in the sleeveless dresses she's partial to, the movie has something like the lunacy of a W. C. Fields in drag."

In February, *Hairspray* was screened at the Miami Film Festival two weeks before its official world premiere in Baltimore. The night of the Miami screening promised to be memorable. My sister Anna had come from Pittsburgh to surprise me—and what a surprise it was. She had driven the whole way alone without telling me because she knew I would worry. I got so excited and called Glenn. He said, "Don't forget to ask Aunt Anna to stay with Dad while you go to the Baltimore premiere with me."

On Monday Anna and I went shopping to find an outfit for me. I bought a beautiful dress at Burdine's. On the night of the premiere, Glenn hired a limousine to pick up Sharon and Frank Kujan, Glenn's friends from Boca Raton, and then me in Margate. The limousine took us to the Omni Hotel, where Glenn had rented a suite. It was so exciting. Glenn met us when we arrived at the hotel. First, he and I kissed each other before he said, "Mom, there is John Waters. Please be nice to him."

I said, "I beg your pardon? Aren't I nice to all your friends?"

"Yes," he said, and we dropped the subject. I did ask about John's pencil moustache, though. "Yes, Mom, it's real," Glenn assured me.

I said, "My God, he's so skinny. I'd like to put some meat on those bones."

Some of my friends who had known Glenn as a kid thought that John had ruined him, and some of the relatives agreed. But who knows what Glenn would have done if he hadn't gotten into making movies? Maybe some members of the family were ashamed of him, but I loved him and couldn't have cared less what people thought. I only wanted him to be happy and healthy. And John and Glenn had been friends for 25 years, and now they were finally on the brink of success, and I was happy for them both.

We all had a good time at Glenn's hotel suite. We had food and drinks, and then it was time to leave to go to the theater. I got more excited by the minute.

We arrived at the theater, and there was such a big crowd coming toward the limousine that the police asked us to drive around the block a few times until more people went inside. Glenn was nervous, so I said to him, "Not to fear, Mommy is here." We all laughed. A police officer came and escorted Glenn inside, and another officer took Frank, Sharon, and me into the theater. The usher told me to sit in the second seat because the first was for Glenn. I was happy that Glenn would be sitting with me. We were about 10 rows from the front.

Before the movie started, John came out to say a few words, and then he introduced Glenn, who called out, "I brought my mother here with me tonight." Glenn then asked me to stand up and turn around so the people could see me. Everybody applauded, and tears started rolling down my face. I was so overwhelmed with happiness. I was so proud of Glenn. The young lady sitting on my right asked me why I was crying. I told her my tears were ones of joy. It turned out that she was a reporter, so the story ended up in the newspapers.

I truly enjoyed the movie. I laughed so hard that Glenn laughed at *me*. It was the best movie that I had seen in a long time. I loved the dancing, which brought back a lot of memories. It was a wonderful night. After the movie, we all met at Glenn's hotel suite to party again. It was late when the limousine took us home, but I could hardly wait to tell Harris and my sister about the night—one I'll never forget.

We'd made plans to meet in Baltimore two weeks later to go to the world premiere at the Senator Theater. Glenn bought me half a dozen airline tickets so I could fly there along with five guests. He had invited Aunt Doris and "Aunt" Ethel Sullivan to come with me. Ethel was the widow of Tim Sullivan, our police officer friend from

Glenn's childhood years.

Glenn had his friend Buddy, who had a shop on Eastern Avenue, do my hair. Glenn also gave me a pearl tiara to match the pearl necklace and earrings I was wearing. I felt like a celebrity: Buddy told the other customers that I was Divine's mom, and they all stared at me. I felt foolish.

Glenn had made arrangements for a limousine to pick us up and take us to the hotel where he was throwing another party. When we met Glenn at the hotel, he quickly rushed me into the suite's bedroom and said, "I got you a mink coat to wear tonight." The coat was beautiful. I told him I would wear it that night, but he would have to take it back to the store the next day because it was too hot to wear it in Florida. That coat brought back memories of my 40th birthday: Glenn had given me a beautiful silver mink stole with my initials inscribed inside the lapel—and I ended up paying for it!

When we left for the theater, where we would meet up with John Waters and the mayor, the elevator got stuck between floors. Who would've believed it? As we waited for help to arrive,

Aunt Doris, me, and Glenn at Hairspray *premiere*

Glenn worried that we would be late. Finally help came, and we were back on our way. When we got to the Senator, mobs of people were dancing in the street, bands were playing, and people were singing. Glenn was so nervous that I could feel the sweat on his hand when he held mine.

Bernard took Glenn to join John and the mayor, who had Glenn and John write their names and make handprints in the ceremo-

nial cement blocks that grace the front of the theater. The blocks commemorate world premieres of movies made in Baltimore or by Baltimoreans, much as the cement inscriptions in the court of Mann's Chinese Theater in Los Angeles celebrate various stars and premieres. Bruce Crockett was in charge of the ceremonial blocks that night. My 350-pound baby knelt down to put his hand in the cement, but then he couldn't get up. The

television cameras captured Bruce helping Glenn to his feet. For years afterward, anytime Bruce would complain of neck or back pain, his family would say, "It's Divine!"

Inside the theater it was a joyful riot. Women were dressed to the hilt with their high hairdos and early '60s outfits. The ushers seated John Waters' family in the same row with Doris, Ethel, and me. Glenn and John presented Lynda Dee of AIDS Action Baltimore with a check for $10,000.

After the premiere, we proceeded to the Baltimore Museum of Art, where the Hair Hoppers' Ball, the post-movie bash, was being held. There was delicious food, plenty to drink, and a band that played until the wee hours of the morning.

All everyone could talk about was how great the movie was and how wonderful my little Glenny's performance was. Jonathan Ross, one of Glenn's London friends and fans, was there to do interviews and wanted to know if he could interview me as well. Glenn asked me if I'd speak with Jonathan, and I said, "OK, but I've never done an interview before." Jonathan asked me about Glenn's childhood, and tears came to my eyes when I replied, "What mother wouldn't want her

son to be a lawyer or a doctor? But if he is happy making movies, it makes me happy." Glenn introduced me to so many people. Before that night, I had never realized that Glenn had so many fans and friends.

The next day, Doris and I met Glenn and Bernard Jay for lunch at the hotel. Glenn ordered a dozen oysters for himself, plus a few side dishes. We talked and laughed about the premiere and the ball. Bernard and he were making plans to throw a 50th anniversary party for Harris and me there at the hotel the following November.

An hour later, I had to leave to catch a plane back to Florida. Glenn walked to the parking lot with Doris, Ethel, and me. I gave him the mink coat I had worn the night before, and we hugged and kissed and said goodbye. "We'll see you at Easter," I called out. Sadly, that was the last time I ever saw him alive.

Glenn left to go to Chicago, New York, and Los Angeles to do interviews. He and John Waters appeared together on *Good Morning America,* and then Glenn did an interview with Larry King. Glenn called to remind us to watch it. When Larry King asked, "What did your mother think when

John Waters, Pat Moran, and Glenn present check to AIDS Action Baltimore

she found out you were making movies?" Glenn replied, "Mom loved it and encouraged me. And after nine years of not seeing my parents, we turned out to be family again and best of friends." Glenn also mentioned that *Hairspray* was getting good reviews and that John was thinking of making a sequel. It was a wonderful interview, and Harris and I were very proud.

Anne Cersosimo, Glenn's friend from Amsterdam, saw some of Glenn's final cabaret acts that year. "Divine was playing at a club in New York in September 1987," she remembers. "It was a multifloored cabaret, and after the show, Divy was holding court with a bunch of us downstairs in the lounge area. We'd been smoking a good amount of marijuana, and Divy was keeping us all in stitches with his impersonations and comedy routines. I couldn't believe it when someone told me that Eartha Kitt was performing upstairs, and we made plans to go up and see part of her act and see if she would receive us backstage. Our conversation went on longer than expected, until we were surrounded by the crowd leaving Eartha's show. A few minutes later, an unmistakable silhouette appeared in the doorway. It was Eartha, who had heard that Divine was still entertaining friends in the lounge and had come down to say hello to him.

"In December, a friend of mine was in Key West for New Year's Eve. A longtime friend of Divy's and John's from the earliest Baltimore days, he was delighted to see an announcement that Divine was appearing live in one of the clubs in Key West. He excitedly told his then-girlfriend about his famous friend performing just blocks away. They changed their New Year's plans and rang in 1988 with Divine's cabaret act. The girlfriend, a nurse and dietician, watched the 350-plus pound Divy strut and gasp through a lengthy set on a narrow stage, drenched with sweat under blazing Fresnel lights. Her boyfriend was laughing and dancing, just delighting in his friend's performance until the two made their way out into the New Year's morning, their ears ringing from the sound system. She shook her head and said, 'If I've ever seen a man who is a prime candidate for a heart attack, it's Divine.' This was probably his last stage appearance."

Glenn kept his promise to me and made an appointment with a doctor in New York while in town to do *The Merv Griffin Show.* Louie Anderson appeared with him on the show and Merv made the remark, "Did you ever see so much fat on one show?" I burst out laughing. The three of them laughed and joked around. It was a funny show: Glenn told Merv that he was not getting out of the chair to exchange it with Louie Anderson. Merv laughed and said, "I know how you feel," and told him to stay put.

The doctor in New York City told Glenn that because he had an enlarged heart and

was under a lot of stress he should take things easy and go on a diet. Glenn promised that he would start his diet after Easter, when he had a big pool party planned and wouldn't be able to resist all the food. The doctor consented, and they set up an appointment for the week after Easter.

That Friday evening, Glenn called and told me about his conversation with the doctor. I said I thought it would be great if he could lose 150 pounds. He would feel better and live longer and be around to bury Harris and me. I had told him that Harris and I had made our burial plans, I had put the contracts in the vault, and we would talk about it when he came home. He thought it was a good idea. Then Glenn said, "Mom, I want you to make Easter baskets for my friends." He said he loved Harris and me, then added, "Don't forget the Easter baskets." Those were the last words I ever heard him say to me: "Don't forget the Easter baskets."

"Things were going incredibly well for Divine," remembers Belle Zwerdling. "He was making a very successful round of the talk shows, and the reviews for *Hairspray* were great. The old stories that Bernard had told me about talk show hosts like Tom Snyder insisting that Div come on the set in drag were not repeating again.

"In February, just as *Hairspray* was going into release, I had called Ronnie Leavitt at

Married With Children to ask if he would consider writing a male role for Divine. At this point, *Married With Children* was one of Fox's top-rated shows, and it was in the Sunday night lineup, which also included some of the new network's most artistically ambitious shows like *It's Garry Shandling's Show, Tracey Ullman* (which later spawned *The Simpsons*), and the romantic comedy, *Duet.* We thought it would be the perfect showcase to bring Div's talent as a character actor to a wider audience and one that would appreciate the edgier aspects of Divy's career and persona. Also, Brandon Tartikoff at NBC was actually talking to us about a TV series for Div."

Steve Friedman also remembers this period. "My favorite time with Divy ever was right after *Hairspray* came out," he says. "All the reviews were favorable. Even those who didn't care for the movie praised his performance. Here he was, sitting in this wonderful penthouse overlooking the Hudson River—his first really magnificent apartment. He had finally arrived. He was a major celebrity in Manhattan. *Interview* magazine had just had him on the cover. Hoofing around Manhattan with him was always fun, but at that time, he was 10 feet tall."

Interview had always been hugely supportive of Glenn's and John's careers, and this final interview with Glenn did a great job in portraying him as a talented actor. The first picture accompanying the article is of Glenn in his "work clothes," a spangled, sequined gown with the full tummy and falsie padding and a huge, teased wig. He's looking over his shoulder with a hand on his hip like Jayne Mansfield. On the opposite page, he is wearing a sport coat, slacks, turtleneck sweater, and a fedora. He's holding a pipe in his left hand and laughing. He almost looks like he is having an affectionate laugh at the expense of the insane-looking creature on the opposite page.

In the interview, he is very candid about the difference between the real person and the crazy star image, explaining how he joined the shoot of *Hairspray* two weeks into production and realized that everyone was terrified of him for a couple of days until they figured out that he wasn't a demented Dawn Davenport. He also shared some of his career plans. "I always admired Sydney Greenstreet. I think he and Charles Laughton left a void there that I can fill. I am not saying that I am as good as they were—they were great actors—but maybe someday I will be. I enjoyed playing Mr. Hodgepile in *Hairspray*, turning into an awful pervert and looking down little girl's dresses."

He was also very honest about some of his personal struggles. "I am a compulsive shopper. The first year I made money, I became addicted to Maud Frizon shoes. I don't eat while I shop, mind you, because it's not nice to get crumbs on the carpet at Bergdorf's. I was also addicted to marijuana. I thought the marijuana was helping me, because it's no fun getting home from a show

150

at 3 A.M. and not being able to fall asleep until five. But soon I found I was stoned all day until I passed out. I started staying at home all the time because I didn't want to end up out in a club somewhere snoring. I didn't care about my career, my looks. It certainly didn't help my weight. When I was stoned, I only ate once a day, but the meal lasted 24 hours. I had agents and managers fighting to create a career for me, and my attitude was, 'Fuck it, let's smoke.' I became difficult to work with, and I had always prided myself on being so professional. I wasn't happy.

"Finally, I realized that I had to do something. But it had to be on my own. I didn't want to go to a clinic only to be released and smoke my brains out. So I went to Malta, where I usually go in the summer, and spent a long time by myself. I did all the corny things: counted my blessings, recalled the bad times when I was on welfare, recalled the good times—like the fight scene in *Lust in the Dust* where I couldn't say my lines because Lainie's tits were in my face; and admitted that I was throwing away a good life."

He described his most recent project: "I just finished a film for Paul Bartel called *Out of the Dark* with Karen Black, Lainie Kazan, Tab Hunter, and the whole bunch from *Lust in the Dust,* and I loved it."

Out of the Dark, which was not released until a year after Glenn's death, is a low-budget thriller about a serial killer who wears a clown mask and is killing off, one by one,

the women who work at a phone sex business. Glenn plays Langella, a foulmouthed homicide detective on the trail of the killer. He sports a huge mustache, which almost completely covers his mouth, and wears a rumpled suit and fedora hat. The credits promise a "special appearance by Divine as Langella," but he doesn't show up until an hour or so into the film, and then only in one scene, where a prostitute's dismembered body is discovered in a hotel bathtub. The movie is a little too close to the *Halloween* type of murder movies for my taste, but it does show Glenn as one of a cast of recognizable character actors in key roles.

When the movie came out on video, the box description suggested that Glenn was one of the leading players, which he clearly wasn't. The review in *Variety,* which didn't like the film at all, pointed out that the "film is notable for cult buffs as the last vehicle for Divine, the 'male actress' of several John Waters pics, who recently passed away. Divine's appearance as Detective Langella is so fleeting as to disappoint anyone but the most hardcore fans." Still, the film ends, after all the credits have rolled by, with the words "In Loving Memory of DIVINE."

"This was such a wonderful time for Divine," remembers Greg Gorman. "He was finally making some money, and nobody liked to spend money more than Divine. He would max out credit cards to buy gifts for his friends, running up bills he could never pay. But he was just such a generous person.

sessions with him out of drag in his wool suit. The shoot was just fabulous. We got some great pictures, and he looked and felt great.

"I spent the last weekend with Divine. He was in Los Angeles for the *Married With Children* shoot. He came straight to my place from the airport and just hung out. He was a huge fan of movie stars and could be just like a little kid. That afternoon, I was doing a shoot with Michael J. Fox to promote *Bright Lights, Big City*. Divine came by that afternoon and sat out by the pool. We went to dinner that night at Bill Travilla's house, who had done a

So many celebrities were never very generous and just so fucking cheap, and Divine was so generous. I always got Christmas presents, and I always got birthday presents. And as a photographic subject, he was one of the best I ever had. He was extremely creative and inventive, always trying to be more outrageous than the time before. He was constantly pushing the buttons, trying to make the most out of any props we had on hand and egging on any people posing with him to match his energy and wit. In the last few months, when he'd lost a lot of weight, we did a couple of

lot of the wardrobe for Marilyn Monroe. That was Saturday night. Sunday night, we went to dinner at City Restaurant in L.A. I took him back that night to his hotel, the Plaza Regency Suites, and left him to go back to my car. When I got down to the courtyard, I turned around, and there he was on his balcony singing, 'Arrivederci, Roma' to me in his big black caftan."

CHAPTER 8

Not now, but in the coming years

It may be in the better land.
We'll read the meaning of our tears,
And there, sometime, we'll understand.

We'll know why clouds instead of sun
Were over many a cherished plan,
Why song has ceased that scarce begun
'Tis there, sometime, we'll understand.

—James McGranahan, "Sometime We'll Understand" (1919)

Sadly, Glenn's train derailed just as it was picking up speed. It was March 7, 1988. I had promised to do a neighbor's hair, and I had left my niece Martha with Harris. While at the neighbor's house an hour or so later, I received a call from Martha telling me to come home. My first thought was that something had happened to Harris. I was only three blocks away, and I rushed home to see what was the matter. Harris, Martha, and another neighbor were there when I arrived. Martha said, "Uncle Harris, you tell her."

Harris made me sit down. And then he told me that Bernard Jay had called to tell us that Glenn had died in his sleep from a heart attack. My body went numb. It seemed like

he took a part of me with him.

Anne Cersosimo remembers, "In early March of 1988, *Hairspray* was getting great reviews, and we were all so happy for Divy. The success and serious recognition for his work that he had craved for so long was seemingly within reach. He was making the dizzying round of talk shows and press interviews and, like so many times before, was planning a trip to Europe to relax once all of the fuss was over. I had just spoken to him, and he was going out to California to audition for *Married With Children* in a recurring role. I had booked a plane for a trip to Ibiza, where we were going to spend a month in May. He had put me in charge of the trip. Then I got this phone call."

"God, what if we drop him?"

"It was a Monday morning," recalls Belle Zwerdling. "I got a call from Ronny Leavitt on the *Married With Children* set telling me that Divine was not there. I thought he was joking. This was impossible, I thought. Divine was not just on time. He was always early. 'I'm not joking,' Ronnie said. 'He's not here.'

"'Let me try to figure this out,' I told him. 'I'll call you back.'

"The next call was from Bernard Jay. 'Div's dead,' he said, 'I'm here at the hotel with the body now. I'm not kidding. Could you come over here? I don't know how long it is going to be before the press finds out and starts to show up here.'

"I called Ronnie back and told him that Div had died, and I drove immediately over to the hotel."

"I was in the middle of a photo session for a book jacket on Monday morning," says Greg Gorman. "I got a phone call from a young actor who was staying in the same hotel, and his first comment was, 'Weren't you good friends with Divine?'

"'What do you mean? I had dinner with him last night.'

"'Well, I'm staying in the complex where he lived, and he's dead.'

"'That's not funny,' I said. 'What's going on?'

"'No, I'm telling you, Divine is dead!'

"It just wiped me out. I canceled my shoot and grabbed Rob Platz, my assistant, and we drove immediately to the hotel, which was just a few blocks from my home. Divine was still there. He was in the bedroom. Belle and Bernard were really nervous about getting him out before the press got there. I didn't even go into the bedroom. Rob went in and picked up his jewelry and everything. I didn't want to go in there, because I had such a phenomenal memory of him from the night before singing to me from the balcony. I just didn't want to go there."

"When I went into the bedroom," says Belle, "he had his *Married With Children* script out and opened. There were cast photos on the side of it, and everything was incredibly orderly. It was obvious that he had been studying the script for the shoot the next day. There was such a calmness to his room. I walked over to the bed, and I saw that there was such a serenity to his body. He looked like he was sleeping.

"The doctors had told him that he wasn't supposed to lie down. He knew he was supposed to lean against the bedstead when he went to sleep, to sleep almost in a sitting up position. I looked at him and thought it seemed almost like a conscious decision to say, 'Wow, now I can finally be like everybody else and lie down when I sleep. It will all be OK.' That's how it felt.

"We sat with the body for six hours: Bernard, Greg, Rob, and I. We made so many phone calls, and nobody would send over a coroner. Finally, I turned to Greg and said, 'Hey, didn't you shoot Thomas Noguchi for the dust jacket of his book?' Noguchi was

"If we do, he'll be the first one to laugh."

the coroner who had done the autopsies of Marilyn Monroe and many other Hollywood stars, and Greg had shot him for *Interview* magazine a few years before. I asked Greg if he would call Noguchi at home and get somebody over here, so he did. And in just a little while, a coroner came over and did the exam and pronounced Divy dead. The official cause of death was cardiac arrest while sleeping. Then the five of us put Divy on a gurney and had to carry him downstairs. You know, those bungalow-style L.A. hotels never have an elevator, so we really struggled to get him downstairs without drawing too much attention.

"At one point, Greg asked, 'God, what if we drop him?'

"'If we do, he'll be the first one to laugh,' I replied."

"I have to say," says Greg, "that as much bad press as Thomas Noguchi has gotten over the years, he really came through for Divine. After we got Divy downstairs, we discovered there was only one press person there. We threw a jacket over the guy's camera and started flipping him off and yelling obscenities at him to make sure they couldn't use the footage on TV. So no one got any footage of us getting Divine out of the hotel, which was really great. Divine was such a terrific person and a great friend that he really deserved all the dignity in the world under those circumstances, and I'm glad there weren't any more photographers there.

"I was having a dinner party for Divine the night all of this happened. We just went ahead and had the party. We knew he would never want us to have a dinner party canceled on his behalf, so we put his picture at the head of the table as if he were still there. It was a pretty rough night, but he wouldn't ever have wanted it any other way."

"I was studying at the Strasberg Institute," remembers Jay Bennett. "I was working on a scene with another actor, and right in the middle of our scene, my teacher, David Gideon, cut me off in mid-sentence and suddenly said, 'OK, that's it. We're done now.' It seemed like such a strange thing. I have no idea to this day why he did it. It was still late morning, and I went back to the apartment Divy and I shared at 90th and Broadway. The doorman looked at me as soon as I got there and said, 'Mr. Bennett, is it true? It's all over the news.'

"'Is what true?' I asked.

"'Mr. Milstead passed away in Los Angeles this morning.'

"I got into the elevator in shock. In the time it took for the elevator to get up to our apartment, I just looked up at the top of the elevator as if looking at Div up in the heavens and said out loud, 'What have you done now?' I walked into the apartment, and the red light on the answering machine was flashing. When I checked the message, it was Bernard, whose message simply said, 'This is Bernard. I think you would like to call me in Los Angeles.' My head was spinning."

Mitch Whitehead, Glenn's number 1 fan,

156

remembers hearing the terrible news. "I was at work, and I got a call from a friend telling me what had happened. I got my stuff together and just left for the day.

"There's a canal by where I live in London, and I just sat there for three or four hours, talking to him. Anyone walking by must have thought I was bloody mad. All I did for the next week or month was sit at home and play his music. I just couldn't believe he was gone.

"I was always in love with the character Divine, but I loved him as Glenn Milstead also because he was such an incredibly nice guy. I would have devoted my life to him, not in a sexual way but as a friend. He was a total original. There will never be another Divine. Ever."

That day was hectic with the news on TV, reporters calling, neighbors running in and out of the house expressing condolences. I had never dreamed in a million years that this could happen to us; children are not supposed to go before their parents. It was a nightmare.

Bernard called again later in the day, still in shock, and said he was worried and didn't know what to do, that Glenn didn't have any life insurance and he didn't have any money. I said, "Bernard, stay calm," and I gave him the address of Ruck's Funeral Home in Towson and told him to have

Glenn's body shipped there. I said I would take care of the funeral arrangements and that Harris and I always kept insurance on Glenn. He was relieved. I told him how sorry I felt for him and would give him the phone number of where we would be staying in Towson after we made the reservations.

That night when I went to bed, I cried, and I was bitter, and I asked God, "Why did this have to happen to him? He was so young and he had great plans for his future." I never did go to sleep.

Channel 10 came to house for an interview the next day. They had called, and I told Martha, "Let them come out." Reporters were calling from all over the world that day. Channel 10 came and did the interview with Harris and me and took pictures of the house and the pool that Glenn had had installed. Afterward, they offered to take us to the airport. I really appreciated their offer to help. I kept thinking of Bernard making the arrangements in California to help me. My heart went out to him, and I felt so sorry for him and wished he was with me.

Pat Moran shakes her head when she thinks about those early months of 1988. "It's really hard, because on one hand it seems as if he's been gone for so long, and on the other hand you turn around and just can't believe it. People talk about extended families, and that was what we all were.

Divine's extended family, from top left to right: Chuck Yeaton, Debbie Harry, Pat Moran, Divine, Ken Ingels, Van Smith, Zandra Rhodes, John Waters, and Greer Yeaton

Everybody who worked on those movies for all of those years, our circle in Baltimore and Provincetown—that was our family, and those weeks were the hardest thing I think that any of us has ever had to go through. We were on cloud nine from great reviews for *Hairspray,* and it was unbelievable that he just didn't wake up one day."

"It was a week after the movie had opened," John Waters told me. "I had just left Divine, it seemed. I saw him last at the Odeon Restaurant in New York at the end of our premiere, kissed him on the cheek, put him in a limo, and that was it. The next thing I knew, I was in my office in my apartment and Bernard Jay called and told me. It was like a bad off-Broadway play. The phone started ringing, and I remember Vince Peranio, Van Smith, and Pat Moran came over, and we all just sat around in the bedroom and listened to message after message coming in from all over the world. The answering machine couldn't keep up with all the calls from just about every person we knew in the world. And all the time, the front desk was calling and saying the news teams are going to stay here until you come out. I thought, 'Well let them stay there. I'm not coming out yet.'

"So it was time to plan the funeral, and there was so much to do. It was like we were still making a movie. The press agent for the film had to come down and be the press agent for the funeral. It was on his résumé. I wasn't even flipping out that much because it seemed that it wasn't real, that it was just

another movie. It's better, I guess, that he died a week after the film came out, because at least he had a week to enjoy his success: He knew the movie was a hit and he got good reviews. But it was very, very frustrating to go through all he did for his entire life and have it finally work—and then be over."

Greer Yeaton remembers Glenn's death: "He actually passed away two days before my 15th birthday, and in the middle of all the great publicity for him and everything wonderful that had happened on *Hairspray,* that was like the big shock, you know, going on my birthday to the funeral home. It was pretty tough. And having all the young people he had worked with on *Hairspray* because it was such a young movie made it tougher. This was the first time they were ever really involved with losing anybody—and especially such a presence. I mean, he walked into a room, he was the room. To lose someone like that in their lives, I think, was hard."

After four days, Glenn's body arrived at Ruck's Funeral home. The undertaker told me the delay was because they had to find a larger casket—they finally located one in North Carolina. We had a viewing on Friday from 1 P.M. to 4 P.M. and then 6 P.M. to 8 P.M. The funeral was on Saturday at 2 P.M.

The New Yorker ran an article the following week on the funeral. Reverend Higgenbotham sent me a copy. "There were 10 pallbearers," the article said. "The casket was ice-blue with chrome trim. Divine wore black, and had a small, round mirror encircled with diamonds and rubies pinned to his lapel. His head, without a wig, looked small and bald."

Flowers from Elton John, Whoopi Goldberg, Tab Hunter, and various other stars flanked the walls surrounding Glenn's casket. The floral designs were beautiful. They were from all over the world and sent with love. One arrangement had a pink flamingo on it, which I carried home on the plane to place by the pool in memory of Glenn. Whoopi Goldberg wrote on her floral card, "What good reviews will do to a person." The card from the producers of *Married With Children* read, "If you didn't want the

job, why didn't you just tell us?" Glenn would have loved it. There were so many flowers that we donated them to nursing homes and hospitals.

John Waters said, "The florist still loves him in this town because, you know, a lot of people say, 'In lieu of flowers send money to such-and-such medical cause.' Not Divine. In the case of my death, spend big bucks! Send the biggest flower arrangement you've ever sent. There were people there, fans, who tried to throw themselves into the coffin at the funeral parlor. Do you remember the funeral at the end of Douglas Sirk's *Imitation of Life* where the estranged daughter comes back

and throws herself on the back of the hearse and screams, 'Mama, mama, I'm here!'? It was a lot like that. But the one good thing I remember about the funeral on that Saturday: It brought Towson to a standstill. Not a reason to die for, certainly, but this entire town, this little village that hated him when he was a teenager, was now at a complete standstill from all the people coming to pay their respects."

Reverend Higgenbotham presided over the service. In his eulogy, he said, "The tragedy is that Glenn or 'Divine' was cut off just as he was coming into his own—like a flower about to bloom. The world will never see how that flower might have unfolded. Those of us who may have been troubled by Divine's individuality need to be reminded that we live in a world where God never creates any two persons exactly alike. God apparently delights in unlimited variety. Every living thing is actually unique.

"However, we do not always celebrate life as it really is, but are forever seeking carbon copies of ourselves and have little tolerance for those who do not share our ideas or ways. We seem to prefer a god who is more like a big Xerox machine or a laboratory turning out clones of ourselves. When we look back at people like Galileo, Columbus, Darwin, Roger Williams, and Thoreau, we realized that so often those considered 'outrageous' in their time have come to be among our great benefactors.

"God has gone to a lot of trouble to make us individuals. We mean a great deal to God. No power in heaven or on earth is able to prevent the finishing of what God has begun. However brief our years here, we are not finished. Although Glenn's life was cut off at a precious moment, this is not the end."

John Waters gave a moving tribute to his friend. He said, "Divine was a dear friend and my star. He was my Elizabeth Taylor. I could never replace him, and I would never try. I never thought of Divine as a female impersonator. I thought of him as a great character actor that started his career playing a homicidal maniac and ended it playing a loving mother. Which is a pretty good stretch, especially when you're a 300-pound man. Divine and I will be linked together forever, and I'm glad of that. I'm proud of that. All I can say is, I wish he was here making movies with me still, but he's not. And I know that. But at least he's there in all those movies forever."

Reverend Higgenbotham told me recently, "I was astonished at how many people came to pay their final respects to Glenn. There were two groups of people—friends and family members from Towson and the Baltimore area, and Glenn's friends who knew him as Divine. Everyone was very dignified and unselfconscious in their grief. All of the brutality Glenn had endured here years before because of peoples' attitudes was now swept away in this overpowering display of love for him and sadness in his passing.

"Although I didn't realize it at the time, presiding over Glenn's service seemed to make me something of a celebrity. About a month after the funeral, I received a telephone call from a television minister in Denver who was troubled by my presence at Glenn's funeral. He felt it was inappropriate that a person like Divine received the respectful treatment he did. He called to invite me on his program to discuss the issue. 'Reverend,' I asked him, 'did you know that Glenn remained a believing Christian all of his life?'

"'Mr. Higgenbotham,' came the reply, 'the homosexual lifestyle and the open promotion of it is incompatible with the Christian faith.'

"'Reverend, are you aware that Glenn was baptized by me as a young man on the same day as his father?'

"'No, I was not aware of this. But—'

"'And do you believe that a baptized Christian is in a state of grace?'

"'Well, certainly, but the sin of homosexuality—'

"'So do you then believe that it is possible for a person to fall from the state of grace

given to them by God in baptism?'

"There was a long silence on the other end of the line. 'I would be happy,' I continued, 'to relive this simple discussion for your television audience.'

"'I do not think that will be necessary, Mr. Higgenbotham,' he replied. We chatted amiably for another minute or two and bid each other goodbye. I do not believe that I heard from him again, nor did I ever hear of his mentioning Glenn on his television program."

I have never been to another funeral where so many came to pay their respects to the departed. And on top of that, there were reporters and photographers from all over the world. Limousines lined Route 1 from the funeral parlor to the cemetery a mile away.

Katey Sagal from *Married With Children* attended the funeral along with the cast from *Hairspray*. Ricki Lake called me "Grandma." That was the first time I had ever been called "Grandma." On her floral card, she wrote, "Mama's little girl Tracy." Jerry Stiller and Anne Meara also came to pay their respects. Unfortunately, my memory of all the people I met at Glenn's funeral has begun to fail me. I can't quite recall everything that happened and the many wonderful people who shared their memories of Glenn with me. But I appreciated the incredible outpouring of love.

Glenn's dear friends and family carried him to his final resting place in Prospect Hill Cemetery. The pallbearers were John Waters, Bernard Jay, Chuck and Brook Yeaton, Andrew Logan, Frank Kejan, and cousins Lee and Barry Milstead. Honorary pallbearers were Harvey Freed, Max Hager, Frank Piazza, Howard Gruber, Phillip Miller, Bob Applegart, Larry Ligoste, and Richard Irea. God bless them all. Reverend Higgenbotham said a prayer at the graveside, and we left Glenn to rest with his grandparents, whom he loved dearly. As a final, fitting tribute, Harris and I decided to put "Divine" on Glenn's headstone next to his dates and given name.

The obituaries for Glenn that appeared in newspapers and magazines all remembered *Pink Flamingos* and noted how far Glenn had come as an actor by starring in a mainstream hit movie like *Hairspray*. Glenn's friend Michael Musto of *The Village Voice* said that Glenn's ultimate "award was the knowledge that he'd offended all the wrong people and inspired all the right ones." Vincent Canby wrote in *The New York Times,* "Divine, the icon of the cinema of John Waters, died suddenly last week in Hollywood, and just as his singular talent was being widely recognized. Though he always resisted being identified as a female impersonator, it's what he did best as an increasingly self-assured actor. His barrel shape, teetering precariously atop high heels, defined Mr. Waters's risky comic method as much as any other image."

As Glenn's parents, Harris and I were proud of his achievements. He gave us a lot of heartaches, and there were some who disapproved of him, but I can only say this to those people: It was our gain and your loss. Just a couple of years after his death, I was in Bible class at church during the ridiculous boycott of Walt Disney World dreamed up by some loudmouthed preacher. People were picketing against gays outside the park, and I told the people in my class how silly I thought that was. Some of them looked up at me in surprise, and then I *proudly* announced that I was Divine's mom.

After the funeral John Waters and Pat Moran invited the family and friends to a beautiful tribute held at the Governors Mansion in Baltimore. Delicious food and drinks were served, and everyone got acquainted. It was just lovely. I thank Pat and John from the bottom of my heart.

When Harris and I arrived home, there was a $10,000 check from the Screen Actors Guild. I called Bernard to tell him the good news, and his reply was, "Your son was the biggest damn liar I ever met." This upset me. Then, a week after the funeral, I received a phone call from the IRS telling me they were coming to my house to take Glenn's possessions to cover the $5,000 in taxes he owed. I told the man that this was Glenn's parents' house and that Glenn had lived in New York. I gave him Bernard's phone number. I remembered the day that Bernard came to our house and told Harris and me that Glenn didn't have any bills or

BY: PATRICK SANDOR, *THE BALTIMORE SUN*

Pallbearers John Waters and Brook Yeaton

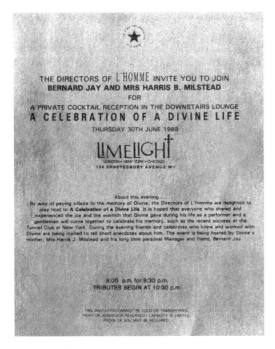

THE DIRECTORS OF L'HOMME INVITE YOU TO JOIN
BERNARD JAY AND MRS HARRIS B. MILSTEAD
FOR
A PRIVATE COCKTAIL RECEPTION IN THE DOWNSTAIRS LOUNGE
A CELEBRATION OF A DIVINE LIFE
THURSDAY 30TH JUNE 1988

LIMELIGHT
LONDON • NEW YORK • CHICAGO
136 SHAFTESBURY AVENUE W1

About this evening....
By way of paying tribute to the memory of Divine, the Directors of L'Homme are delighted to
play host to A Celebration of a Divine Life. It is hoped that everyone who shared and
experienced the joy and the warmth that Divine gave during his life as a performer and a
gentleman will come together to celebrate his memory, such as the recent success at the
Tunnel Club in New York. During the evening friends and celebrities who knew and worked with
Divine are being invited to tell short anecdotes about him. The event is being hosted by Divine's
mother, Mrs Harris J. Milstead and his long time personal Manager and friend, Bernard Jay

9:00 p.m. for 9:30 p.m.
TRIBUTES BEGIN AT 10:00 P.M.

THIS INVITATION CANNOT BE SOLD OR TRANSFERRED
RIGHT OF ADMISSION RESERVED / CAPACITY IS LIMITED
PROOF OF AGE MAY BE REQUIRED

worries. What a surprise!

Jay Bennett says, "The whole issue of what Divy had given to people or received from people turned into a real mess. A lot of stuff that was sold at the Christie's auction in November 1988 really should have been donated to the Wesleyan Archives where John Waters has his papers kept. There were these gorgeous Van Smith gowns that Divy had worn on his disco tours that ended up in the possession of wealthy fans. They really should be in a museum somewhere. I went to the auction and had to buy back some of my own stuff there, so I was pretty upset."

We'll probably never know what really belonged to whom. Bernard did take care of Glenn's taxes, though. And in May, a few months after the funeral, he gave a tribute to Glenn at the Tunnel, a New York City disco. It was beautiful, and I met a lot of Glenn's fans and friends.

When Easter came, the pool was finished. Bernard, Steve, Sharon, and Frank spent Easter with us. We had a delicious meal: We laughed and cried. It was a sad occasion.

On June 30, 1988, Donald McKay and Jim Schnee gave a tribute to Glenn at the Limelight nightclub in London. They bought me an airline ticket and paid for my hotel stay for a week. It was my first trip to England. My niece Martha traveled with me. The tribute was titled "A Celebration of Divine's Life." I couldn't take my eyes off the architecture in London and all of the blue, green, and purple hairdos. Everything was fascinating—even the people driving on the wrong side of the road!

At the Limelight, they showed video clips from *Women Behind Bars, Down and Dirty Divine* (which had been shot at the Hippodrome), *Hairspray, Female Trouble,* and *Out of the Dark,* Glenn's last screen appearance. With tears in my eyes and shaking in my shoes as Bernard tried to keep me calm, I went to the podium and thanked everyone for attending. After the tributes, the music played, and everyone started dancing. Ricki Lake and her mom were there with Michael St. Gerard from *Hairspray.* It was a glorious evening.

In November Glenn's things were auc-

tioned at Christie's in New York. Bernard had made the arrangements, but had to go to Europe and wasn't with me at the sale. Mink Stole, Mitch Whitehead, and Jay Bennett accompanied me. While I was staying in New York, I received a call from the IRS telling me they would meet me at

Christie's so I could sign papers giving them the right to the money made on the sale of Glenn's possessions. It was a sad time for us. The Andy Warhol paintings were *not* sold at the auction.

Mink Stole treated us all to dinner at an Italian restaurant afterward, and then we

At Christie's auction with Mitch Whitehead and Mink Stole

went to my hotel room where we sat, talked, and drank Cokes until the early morning hours. I remembered Mink saying, "Fran, I wish my mother was as broad-minded as you are." I laughed and told her that all mothers probably think differently. We had a great time together, and the next day I went back to Florida.

Glenn's final resting place is Prospect Hill Cemetery in Towson, Maryland, just a few blocks from where he grew up and just a couple of hundred feet from where he worked at James Hair Salon, where he first looked me in the eye and said, "I'm a star."

Glenn's dad joined him just five years later. A few years ago when I was visiting Glenny's grave, I was surprised to find lipstick kisses smeared on the headstone. I thought this was disrespectful, and I spoke to the cemetery's director. He told me the grounds crew finds things at Glenn's grave every day. He told me of fans leaving Glenn notes, articles of women's clothing, and plastic pink flamingos stuck into the ground near the headstone! I have come to see these little tributes left at my son's grave as just that. Every year, John Waters and Pat Moran bring a small decorated Christmas tree to the cemetery for the holidays.

I think Glenn would want us to remember him as a fun-loving, gentle, and giving person. He's helped gays come out of the closet; he's even helped heavy-set people feel good about themselves. His life message was "Be whatever you are and live life to the fullest." Glenn gave us a lot of memories, a lot of laughs—and a lot of love. And I feel we should all cherish those memories.

Glenn will live on in the hearts of the people who knew him. Brook Yeaton, his godson, told me, "Divine was probably the most loving person whom I have ever met in my entire life. If I wrote a dictionary and it had Brook Yeaton's definition of love, it would have a picture of Divy next to it saying, 'The way he treated me.'"

Just a couple of years ago, John Waters told an interviewer that the field in Phoenix, Maryland, where the house trailer scenes in *Pink Flamingos* were shot is now a suburban housing development. He hoped that Divine's spirit is still there, giving strength and courage to the misunderstood and tormented kids in the neighborhood. Amen, John. Amen.

FILMOGRAPHY

Roman Candles (1966)
8-millimeter short directed by John Waters
Approximately 38 minutes
(Guest at birthday party)
with Bob Skidmore, Mink Stole, Mary Vivian
Pearce, David Lochary, and Maelcum Soul

Eat Your Makeup (1967)
16-millimeter short directed by John Waters
45 minutes
(Jackie Kennedy)
with Mary Vivian Pearce, David Lochary,
Mona Montgomery, and Maelcum Soul

Mondo Trasho (1969)
16-millimeter feature directed by John Waters
94 minutes
(Divine)
with David Lochary, Mary Vivian Pearce, and
Mink Stole

The Diane Linkletter Story (1969)
16-millimeter short directed by John Waters
Approx. 35 minutes
(Diane Linkletter)
with David Lochary and Mary Vivian Pearce

Multiple Maniacs (1970)
16-millimeter feature directed by John Waters
90 minutes
(Lady Divine)
with Mary Vivian Pearce, Edith Massey,
David Lochary, Cookie Mueller, and Paul
Swift

Pink Flamingos (1972)
16-millimeter feature directed by John Waters,
released in 35-millimeter blowup
93 minutes
(Divine/Babs Johnson)
with Mary Vivian Pearce, Danny Mills, Edith
Massey, David Lochary, Mink Stole, Paul
Swift, and Chan Wilroy

Female Trouble (1974)
16-millimeter feature directed by John Waters,
released in 35mm blowup
92 minutes
(Dawn Davenport/Earl Peterson)
with David Lochary, Mary Vivian Pearce,
Edith Massey, and Mink Stole

Tally Brown, New York (1979)
16-millimeter documentary feature directed by
Rosa Von Praunheim
97 minutes
(Himself)
with Tally Brown, Gil Fontaine, Holly Woodlawn, and Taylor Mead

Alternative Miss World (1980)
35-millimeter documentary feature directed by
Richard Gayer
81 minutes
(Guest of honor)
with Andrew Logan, Little Nell, Zandra
Rhodes, Eric Roberts, Richard DeVelasco,
John Thomas, and Rosemary Gibb
(released on home video in 1985 under the
title, *I Wanna Be a Beauty Queen*)

Polyester (1981)
35-millimeter feature directed by John Waters
85 minutes
(Francine Fishpaw)
with Tab Hunter, Mary Garlington, Edith Massey, Stiv Bators, David Samson, Mink Stole, and Ken King

Divine: Live at the Hacienda (taped 1982, released 1994)
Directed by Malcolm Whitehead
75 minutes
(Himself, live in concert)

Divine Waters (1985)
16-millimeter documentary feature directed by Vito Zagarrio
110 minutes
(Himself)
with John Waters, Edith Massey, Tab Hunter, Pat Waters, and John Waters, Sr.

Lust in the Dust (1985)
35-millimeter feature directed by Paul Bartel
85 minutes
(Rosie Velez)
with Tab Hunter, Lainie Kazan, Woody Strode, Geoffrey Lewis, and Cesar Romero

Trouble in Mind (1985)
35-millimeter feature directed by Alan Rudolph
111 minutes
(Hilly Blue)
with Kris Kristofferson, Keith Carradine, Genevieve Bujold, Lori Singer, George

Kirby, and Joe Morton

Hairspray (1988)
35-millimeter feature directed by John Waters
90 minutes
(Edna Turnblad, Arvin Hodgepile)
with Ricki Lake, Jerry Stiller, Sonny Bono, Deborah Harry, Ruth Brown, Leslie Ann Powers, Shawn Thompson, and Michael St. Gerard

Out of the Dark (1988)
35-millimeter feature directed by Michael Schroeder
89 minutes
(Detective Langella)
with Cameron Dye, Lynn Danielson, Tracey Walter, Karen Black, Bud Cort, Lainie Kazan, and Tab Hunter

Divine Trash (1998)
16-millimeter documentary feature directed by Steve Yeager, released in 35-millimeter blowup
96 minutes
(Himself, archival footage)
with John Waters, Mink Stole, Steve Buscemi, George and Mike Kuchar, Mary Avara, Edith Massey, Jim Jarmusch, David Lochary, Chan Wilroy, and Mary Vivian Pearce

In Bad Taste (1999)
Television documentary feature directed by Steve Yeager
95 minutes

(Himself, archival footage)
with John Waters, Kathleen Turner, Ricki
Lake, Jane and Michael Stern, David Insley,
and Lili Taylor

Divine: The E! True Hollywood Story (1999)
Television documentary feature produced by
Mark A. Harris; editorial director, James
Medlin
100 minutes
(Himself, archival footage)
with John Waters, Frances Milstead, Mel
Scott, Tab Hunter, and Keith Carradine

Tales from the Darkside (1984–)
Television series, (episode 4.8: "Seymour-
lama"), first aired 11/15/87
(Chia Fung)

DISCOGRAPHY

SINGLES

Born To Be Cheap
1979, Wax Trax Records
"Born To Be Cheap"

Shoot Your Shot
1982, "O" Records
"Shoot Your Shot," "Jungle Jezebel"

Love Reaction
1983, "O" Records
Track List: "Love Reaction"

Shake It Up
1983, "O" Records
"Shake It Up," "Shake It Up" (Instrumental)

I'm So Beautiful
1984, Proto Records
"I'm So Beautiful" (Mix), "I'm So Beautiful"
(Divine Mix), "Show Me Around"

You Think You're a Man
1984, Proto Records
"You Think You're a Man" (Extended), "You
Think You're a Man" (Radio Mix), "Give It
Up"

Hard Magic
1985, Proto Records
"Hard Magic," "Hard Magic" (Magic Mix),
Hard Magic (Instrumental)

Twistin' the Night Away
1985, Proto Records
"Twistin' the Night Away," "A Divine Good
Time"

Walk Like a Man
1985, Proto Records
"Walk Like a Man" (Extended), "Man Talk,"
"Man Talk" (Cowgirl Version)

Divine Madness
1985, Memo Records
"Divine Madness," "Double-0 Divine"

Hey You!
1987, ZYX Records
"Hey You!" "Hey What!"

Little Baby
1987, Proto Records
"Little Baby" (Extended), "Little Baby"
(Original), Little Baby (Instrumental)

ALBUMS/CDs/EPs

Jungle Jezebel
1997, Hot Records
"Shoot Your Shot," "Jungle Jezebel," "Native
Love," "Kick Your Butt," "Alphabet Rap,"
"Native Love" (Instrumental)

Born to Be Cheap
1995, Chred Records
Recorded Live

"Gang Bang," "Jungle Jezebel," "Born To Be Cheap," "Alphabet Rap," "Native Love," "Shake It Up," "Shoot Your Shot," "Gang Bang," "Shoot Your Shot," "Jungle Jezebel," "Born To Be Cheap," "Love Reaction," "Alphabet Rap," "Shake It Up," "Native Love, "Love Reaction "

The Originals/The Remixes (2-CD set)
1996, Dance Street Records
Volume 1:
"Shoot Your Shot," "Jungle Jezebel," "Native Love," "Love Reaction," "Shout It Out," "T-shirts and Tight Blue Jeans," "Psychedelic Shack," "Shake It Up," "Kick Your Butt," "Alphabet Rap"
Volume 2:
"Shoot Your Shot" (Jon of the Pleased Wimmin Remix), "Jungle Jezebel" (Hyper Go-go Remix), "Native Love" (John of the Pleased Wimmin Remix), "Love Reaction" (Jon of the Pleased Wimmin Remix), "Shout It Out" (Checkpoint Charlie Remix), "T-shirts and Tight Blue Jeans" (Checkpoint Charlie Remix), "Psychedelic Shack" (Hybrid remix), "Shake It Up" (Aquarius Remix), "Kick Your Butt" (Hybrid Remix), "Alphabet Rap" (Hyper Go-go Remix), "Native Love" (Mark Moore Remix)

Greatest Hits
1994, Unidisc Records
"Native Love" (Remix), "Shake It Up," "Love Reaction," "Jungle Jezebel," "Shoot Your Shot," "Kick Your Butt," "Alphabet Rap,"

"Native Love"
The Story So Far
1994, Receiver Records
"Native Love," "Shake It Up," "Shoot Your Shot," "Love Reaction," "Jungle Jezebel," "Alphabet Rap"

The Cream of Divine
1994, Pickwick Group
"You Think You're a Man," "Walk Like a Man," "Love Reaction," "Jungle Jezebel," "Native Love," "I'm So Beautiful," "Man Talk," "Alphabet Rap," "Shoot Your Shot," "Give It Up"

12" Mixes
1993, Unidisc Records
"Native Love" (Remix), "Shoot Your Shot," "Shake It Up," "Love Reaction," "Psychedelic Shack," "Shout It Out," "Jungle Jezebel," "Kick Your Butt, Alphabet Rap, "T-shirts and Tight Blue Jeans," "Native Love" (Remix 2), "Native Love"

The Best of Divine
1991, Hot Records
"Shoot Your Shot," "Jungle Jezebel," "Native Love," "Love Reaction," "Shout It Out," "T-shirts and Tight Blue Jeans," "Psychedelic Shack," "Shake It Up," "Kick Your Butt," "Alphabet Rap," "You Think You're a Man," "Walk Like a Man," "I'm So Beautiful," "Hey You!"

Maid in England
1988, ZYX Records
"Divine's Theme," "You Think You're a
Man," "Give It Up," "I'm So Beautiful,"
"Show Me Around," "Walk Like a Man"
(Remix), "Twistin' the Night Away" (Remix),
"Good Time '88," "Hard Magic" (Magic
Mix), "Little Baby" (Remix), "Hey You!"
(Remix), "Divine Reprise," "Hey You!" (The
Trumpet Mix)

You Think You're A... (Medley)
1984, Proto Records
"You Think You're a Man," "Native Love,"
"Walk Like a Man," "Shoot Your Shot,"
"Native Love '84"
Shoot Your Shot
1982, Mastertone Records
"Shoot Your Shot," "Jungle Jezebel," "Native
Love," "Love Reaction," "Shout It Out," "T-shirts
and Tight Blue Jeans," "Psychedelic Shack
1985," "Shake It Up," "Kick Your Butt,"
"Alphabet Rap," "Divine Madness,"
"Psychedelic Shack" (Jungle Beat), "Love
Reaction" (Calypso Version), "Native Love"
(Holland Remix), "Shout It Out" (Montreal
Remix)

The Best of and the Rest of Divine
1989, Action Replay
"Native Love," "Shake It Up," "Shoot Your
Shot," "Love Reaction," "Jungle Jezebel"

COMPILATION CDs
and TRIBUTE ALBUMS

The Definitive 12-Inch Collection (2-CD set)
1990, Hot Records
Featured artists, vol. 1
Gomez Presley, The Flirts, Native Love
(Divine), Waterfront Home, Oh Romeo,
Screamin' Tony Baxter, Miss Kimberly, Eric,
Tony Caso, "O" & Company, I Spies,
Gina Desire
Featured artists, vol. 2
Bobby O, Band Of South, Bonnie Forman,
Hotline, Oh Romeo, Pet Shop Boys, Malibu,
One-Two-Three, Beat Box Boys, Girly,
1 Plus 1, Roni Griffith, Fascination, Barbie &
The Kens
Disco Fox Fever, Vol. 1
1991, DST Records
"Touch By Touch," "It Feels Like I'm in Love,"
"Show Me the Way to Your Heart," "It's Been
So Long," "Rock Your Baby," "I Can't Leave
You Alone," "Dream of Great Emotion,"
"You're My Heart You're My Soul," "You Spin
Me Round," "Coat Of Many Colors," "I'd Love
You to Want Me," "Living Next Door to Alice,"
"Needles & Pins," "Stumblin' In," "For a Few
Dollars More," "If You Think You Know How,"
"Living Next Door to Alice," "Mexican Girl,"
"Out of the Blue," "Sun of Jamaica," "Just
Can't Get Enough," "Lover Why," "Blue Alice,"
"Love Boat," "Shoot Your Shot" (Divine),
"Pump Up the Jam," "Macho Man"

Black Box: Wax Trax (3-CD set)
1994, Wax Trax Records
Featured artists, vol. 1:
1000 Homo DJs, Revolting Cocks, Sister Machine Gun, Excessive Force, Young Gods, Pailhead, Lead Into Gold, Front Line Assembly, Mussolini Headkick, Greater Than One, Pig, Hope & Kirk, Wreck, Strike Under
Featured Artists, vol. 2:
Chris Connelly, Coil, Clock DVA, KMFDM, Ministry, A Split Second, Foetus, Doubting Thomas, Cyberaktif, Controlled Bleeding, In the Nursery
Featured Artists, vol. 3:
PTP, Acid Horse, KLF, Psykosonic, My Life With the Thrill Kill Kult, Laibach, Meat Beat Manifesto, Fred, Psychic TV, Pankow, Divine ("The Name Game")

'80s Dance Party, Vol. 2
1994, SPV Records
X-Posed, Timex Social Club, Nenah Cherry, Bananarama, File 13, Dominatrix, Joyce Sims, Divine ("You Think You're A Man"), Hashim, Cameo, Bronski Beat, Strafe

Best Disco in Town (2-CD set)
1995, Hot Records
Featured artists, vol.1:
Van McCoy & The Soul City Symphony, Santa Esmeralda, The Ritchie Family, Arpeggio, Silver Convention, Kongas, Carol Douglas, Bazuka, Celi Bee & The Buzzy Bunch, George Kranz, Frankie Smith, Eartha Kitt, Julius Brown, Disco Tex & His Sex-O-Lettes, Sylvia, Cheri, Queen Samantha, Tony

Valor Orchestra, Phyllis Nielson
Featured artists, vol. 2:
Roni Griffith, Pet Shop Boys, Wish, Earlene Bentley, Pattie Brooks, El Coco, Rice & Beans Orchestra, Estination, M. Machine, T-Connection, Voyage, Claudja Barry, The Flirts, Bobby 'O,' Divine ("Native Love"), Dvelyn Thomas, Miquel Brown, Louise Thomas, Carol Jiani

Kool Hits of the '80s
1995, Avex Records
"Nothing's Gonna Stop Me Now," "So Many Men," "Give Me Up," "Unexpected Lovers," "Boom Boom," "Carry On," "Mickey," "Bump," "If U Keep It Up," "Native Love" (Divine), "She's Playing Hard To Get," "It's All In Mr. Magic"

Back Into the 80s, Vol. 2
1995, Hart Records
"Last Night a DJ Saved My Life," "Let the Music Play," "Dirty Ol' Man," "Passion," Pop Music, Saddle Up, You Sexy Thing, That's the Way, Spank," "I'm On Fire," "Love Me Like a Lover," "Shoot Your Shot" (Divine), "I Can't Leave You Alone," "In the Navy"

Crossroads
1996, Pro D.J. Records
Car Wash, Disco Mixes, Hit That Perfect Beat, Lady Marmalade, You Think You're A Man" (Divine), "Real Wild House, House Is Our Music," I Remember, We Are Family '98, One, Disco Rouge, Love & Peace, Dance Dance Dance, I Love My Radio,

Music, Peace Train, Down Town, Don't Talk
To Me About Love, Stop, My Heart Will Go
On, Together, Key Of Life, Frozen, This Is
My Life, I Feel Love, House Your Body,
Don't Go, Just Can't Help Believing,
Smalltown Boy, So Addicted

High Energy, Vol. 2 (2-CD set)
1996, Hot Records
Featured artists, vol. 1:
Lisa, Paul Parker, Erotic Drum Band, Jimmy
Ruffin, Bobby 'O,' Divine ("Shoot Your
Shot"), Boys Town Gang, The Flirts, Jigsaw,
Barbara Pennington, Club Shott, Seventh
Avenue, Moonstone, Eve, Evelyn Thomas,
Oh Romeo, Waterfront Home
Featured artists, vol. 2:
Angie Gold, Marsha Raven, Laura Pallas,
Pearly Gates, Carol Jiani, Hazell Dean,
Norma Lewis, Phyllis Nelson, Louise
Thomas, Tony Casso, Break Machine,
Earlene Bentley, Lydia Steinman, Sadie
Nine, Kelley Marie, Margaret Reynolds,
Bassix, Company B

Disco Gold (3-CD set)
1997, Riviere International Records
Featured artists, vol. 1:
Paul Hardcastle, Crazy Coons, Disco Circus,
Carl Douglas, Lisa Cult, Gloria Gaynor,
Miquel Brown, Evelyn Thomas, Heatwave,
Sabrina, Tina Charles, Delegation, Hot
Chocolate, Stephanie
Featured artists, vol. 2:
Shalamar, Gwen McCrae, The Flirts,

Bohannon, Shirley & Company, Carol
Douglas, Indeep, KC & the Sunshine Band,
Timmy Thomas, Jocelyn Brown, Claudja
Barry, Houston Cover, Sylvester,
Divine ("Love Reaction")
Featured artists, vol. 3:
Kool & The Gang, LaToya Jackson, Tina
Charles, The Flirts, Donna Summer, The
Nolans, Jefra Concept, L.A. Mix, Motor City
All-Stars, Rififi, Timmy Thomas, Fay Yourself,
Geraldine Hunt, Kool & The Gang

The Best of "O" Records, Vol. 1
1997, Hot Records
Roni Griffith, The Flirts, Bobby 'O,' Bobby
'O' & Claudja Barry, Barbie & the Kens,
Divine ("Native Love"), Free Enterprise,
Oh Romeo, Divine ("Love Reaction"),
Gomez Presley, Hot Line, Band of South, The
Flirts

The Best of "O" Records, vol. 2
1997, Hot Records
The Flirts, Divine ("Shoot Your Shot"), Malibu,
Waterfront Home, Girly, Roni Griffith, Eric,
Bobby 'O,' Oh Romeo, Pet Shop Boys

Klone Ikons
1997, Klone Records
"Wicked Game," "Take My Breath Away,"
"Could It Be Magic," "In the Name of Love,"
"S.O.S," "Classical Gas," "Native Love"
(Divine), "Love in the Shadows," "Sunny"
(Squeezy Lemon Mix), "Sunshine After The
Rain," "One More Hurt," "Jolene" (Nashville

Mix), "Losing My Religion," "Drive," "P.A.S.S.I.O.N.," "U Know It's Good" (4 U Mix), "Constant Craving," "In My Wildest Dreams," "Hills of Katmandu," "Wonderful Life," "Finger of Suspicion," "With or Without You," "Don't Tell Me Why" (Remix), "Feels Like a Dream," "Smells Like Teen Spirit," "Runaway Train" (Clubola Mix), "Don't Go," "You Know I Want You," "Visitors," "Take Me Higher," "Inside," "Dance With the Devil," "Paradise Medley," "Eat You Up," "Sailing," "A Girl Like You," "Riders On the Storm," "Fame," "Delirious," "Do It To Me," "This Wheel's on Fire," "I Will Do Anything," "Music Is My Life," "High on Love," "I'm on a Love Train," "Chase" (The Oxygene Mix)

Disco Nights, Vol. 4
1998, Unidisc Records
"Knock On Wood," "Love Is In The Air," "Kung Fu Fighting," "Dance Little Lady Dance," "I Love Music," "Shame," "Rasputin," "I've Got The Next Dance," "Dance" (Disco Heat), "Woman In Me," "Get Up and Boogie (That's Right)," "Act Like You Know," "You to Me Are Everything," "My Simple Heart," "Beat Goes On," "She Can't Love You," "Night To Remember," "Boys Will Be Boys," "Native Love" (Divine), "Guilty"

Glad To Be Gay, Vol. 1
1997, SPV Records
"Don't Leave Me This Way," "You Make Me Feel" (12" Ultimix), "Smalltown Boy,"

"Tainted Love," "Shoot Your Shot" (Divine), "High Energy," "I Am What I Am," "Crucified," "Do You Really Want to Hurt Me," "I Love Men," "Heaven in Pain," "Where Is My Man?," "I'm Too Sexy," "You Think You're a Man" (Divine), "Boogie Woogie Dancin' Shoes," "Persuasion"

Glad To Be Gay, Vol. 2
1998, SPV Records
"Why???" (Original Mix), "Can't Take My Eyes off of You" (Hot Tracks Mix), "West End Girls" (Original Mix), "Knock on Wood (Remix), "I'm on Fire" (Furnace Mix), "Power of Love" (Club Mix), "Deep in My Heart," "Somebody Else's Guy," "Wind Beneath My Wings," "Love Reaction" (Divine), "Angel Lies Sleeping" (Spanish Radio Encore), "Make Up," "Fly to Me" (Fly Version), "Isn't It Romantic?"

Glad to Be Gay, Vol. 3
1998, SPV Records
"Heartbeat," "I Believe," "Hands Up for Lovers," "It's Raining Men," "Blame it on the Boogie," "Let Me Be Your Underwear," "Sex Dwarf," "I'm So Beautiful" (Divine), "In the Navy," "Legendary Children," "Free Gay and Happy," "Lover Come Back to Me," "She Drives Me Crazy," "Walk on the Wild Side," "Rumpelstilzchen"

Queer As Folk, Vol. 2
2000, Chan4 Records
"Haven't You Heard," "Sway," "Gonna
Catch You Baby, Real Thing," "Relight My
Fire," "Can't Take My Eyes off of You," "You
to Me Are Everything," "Sometimes,"
"Dancing Queen" (Millenium Mix), "Never
Gonna Give You Up," "Love Come Down,"
"Get Down on It," "Walk Like a Man"
(Divine Remix), and many other songs

AUTHOR BIOGRAPHIES

Frances Milstead is retired and living in Florida. She is an active member of several civic and religious groups, and she has been very active on behalf of a number of causes of interest to the gay and lesbian community. Recently, she was interviewed in the E! Channel documentary on Divine's life for which the filmmakers received a Lambda Image Award. This is her first book.

Kevin Heffernan is Assistant Professor of Cinema in the Meadows School of the Arts at Southern Methodist University in Dallas, where he teaches courses in screenwriting, film history, and 16-millimeter film production. He was cowriter and associate producer with Steve Yeager for the documentary features about John Waters, *Divine Trash* and *In Bad Taste.* He lives in Dallas with his wife and daughter and has just completed a book on horror films of the '50s and '60s.

Steve Yeager has been active as a stage director and filmmaker for over 25 years. In addition to cowriting and directing *Divine Trash,* the 1998 Sundance Film Festival Best Documentary winner about the early career of cult director John Waters, Yeager directed the late Howard E. Rollins Jr. in one of his last film roles, *On the Block* (1991) He also cowrote and directed *In Bad Taste,* a feature-length documentary sequel to *Divine Trash,* for the Independent Film Channel/Bravo. Most recently, he completed a feature film adaptation of Jack Gelber's play, *The Connection,* a remake of Shirley Clarke's 1961 film. He lives and teaches in Baltimore.